CONTENTS

CAREER WORK EXPERIENCE

A Career Development Workbook

Third Edition
Revised Printing

Diane S. Taylor

Consultant, Coordinator and Instructor,
Career Work Experience

Maricopa County Community Colleges
Phoenix, Arizona

Illustrated by
Bil Dambrova

[handwritten: Highlight Points of Interest Due on 9/24/10.]

KENDALL/HUNT PUBLISHING COMPANY
4050 Westmark Drive   Dubuque, Iowa 52002

Copyright © 1989, 1992, 1994, 1999 by Kendall/Hunt Publishing Company

Revised printing 2004

ISBN 978-0-7575-1436-4

Printed in the United States of America
10 9 8

PREFACE

Writing my own textbook was not a part of my career plan when I first became involved in career development a number of years ago. Since that time, I have been fortunate enough to have the opportunity to help thousands of individuals with their career development and planning. It has been very gratifying to me to "see direction" in the eyes of a student who has been confused and unsure about himself/herself in relation to the world of work. I have also had the privilege of seeing excitement and motivation from students who are "reality testing" a work environment and gaining skills and experience.

I have wanted to help my students with their career development in the best way possible. Therefore, I developed a variety of course materials that presented career planning in a logical, helpful manner. After giving a great number of handouts to my students over the years, it became a logical idea to attempt the writing of my own textbook. Thus, I became the author of your *Career Work Experience* text to be used for a course that offers career exploration, on-the-job training, work experience and career development.

It is my intention that this text serve as a supplement to the *Career Work Experience* weekly seminars, giving you a complete foundation for your career development. Included in this text is a self-assessment, aimed at answering the question "Who am I?" in relation to the world of work. Setting career goals encourages you to formulate a plan or strategy to achieve your career objective. Job hunting strategies, writing a winning resume and interviewing all set the stage toward getting your targeted job. The section on career pathing and future trends gives you the opportunity to see into and prepare for the future . . . your future. It is my hope that the class seminars, coupled with the supplemental information from this text, will guide you toward a meaningful and satisfying career.

ACKNOWLEDGMENTS

I have a genuine appreciation for those who contributed in a variety of ways toward the writing of this textbook.

I am appreciative of the patience and support that my children, Lana, Jill and Eric, have shown me throughout my career.

I am indebted to Dr. Renee Rodgers-Barstack, Director of Career Services at Glendale Community College, Glendale, Arizona for her inspiration, encouragement and never-ending support of me and the *Career Work Experience* program. She has been both a strong force behind my career and, also, a friend.

A thank you is extended to Liz Harris-Tuck, Career Consultant, for her wonderful capacity to listen and share.

I am also grateful for the administrators who recognized the potential and importance of this program and have given their support.

Diane S. Taylor

INTRODUCTION

Our lives are filled with constant changes, both from the outside world and from the inner world within each of us. Changes in the economy can result in unexpected business takeovers, lay-offs, or a recession—each of which has the potential to compel us to make career changes. Our inner world may experience a change in values and priorities. Our interests may also change, leaving us with a lack of enthusiasm and sense of challenge toward a particular job. Because of our changing world, the average worker may experience as many as ten jobs in a lifetime and two or more changes in career direction. The only thing that is certain in our lives is change. Career planning allows us to expect, accept and plan for change. It includes learning about ourselves in relationship to the world of work and provides us with the tools for making good career decisions.

The text *Career Work Experience: A Career Development Workbook* is designed to assist you in your career planning and decision making and guide you toward a meaningful and satisfying career. It was also written to be used in conjunction with the *Career Work Experience* course offered by Maricopa County Community Colleges. This unique course offers you the opportunity to plan your career in a logical, meaningful manner. It also allows you to reality test a work environment in order to explore a career and/or gain skills and experience in a given field. This aspect of the course demonstrates the vital relationship between college courses and the real work world. In addition, you will attend a weekly seminar that focuses on your career development.

PURPOSE AND COVERAGE

The purpose of this book is to help you answer the following four questions: "Who am I in relationship to the world of work?", "What options do I have?", "What is the best career for me?", and "How do I get from here to there?". To help you accomplish these goals, it includes the following components:

- ❑ **Self Assessment.** You will assess your values, motivators, priorities, interests, personality and skills to gain an understanding of yourself in relationship to the work world. The focus will be on looking at options that allow you to express your personality, use your favorite skills, and meet your personal needs and values. This can be appropriately labeled the concept of *"person/job fit"*.
- ❑ **Setting career goals.** You will formulate a plan or strategy to help you achieve your career goal(s) in addition to learning about the importance of goal setting.
- ❑ **Job hunting strategies.** You will learn that no one job hunting strategy is the best. The focus will be on a variety of strategies, all of which have the potential to help you land that special job.
- ❑ **Cover letters, resumes, applications and interviews.** You will learn about and become skillful in marketing yourself for your target job. The focus will be on developing your

ability to present information about yourself in the most concise, clear and positive manner. Such skills are critical, as you are engaged in a competitive job hunt.

❑ **Career pathing.** You will learn about the importance of continual planning to help you reach your career goals. The focus will also be on the direction of your career path.

❑ **Trends and predictions.** You will learn how economic and population trends affect the work place and job market and ultimately . . . YOU. The focus will be on being prepared for changes in the work world. The fastest growing occupations and occupations with the largest job growth are highlighted.

LEARNING ENVIRONMENT

The method of teaching skills used in this text involves both presentation of major concepts and information in addition to providing you with exercises to promote your self-discovery, planning and decision making. This method calls for your active involvement.

1. You will reflect upon each component within the self-assessment portion of the text and relate it to the work place.
2. Through the seminars, you will be given the opportunity for group discussion in addition to participating in small group exercises.
3. You will be given the opportunity to assess past information and integrate it with present up-to-date career planning strategies and tools.
4. You will evaluate your career development and growth as a result of the seminars and field experience.

BENEFITS

This program's primary objective is to enhance *your* career development. The course *Career Work Experience* has the potential to:

❑ Give you the opportunity for self-assessment.
❑ Enhance your chances for job satisfaction.
❑ Contribute to your success within a given field.
❑ Enhance your self-marketing skills.
❑ Promote the setting of career goals.
❑ Demonstrate the vital relationship between college courses and the real work world.

It is hoped that the seminars and field work together will enhance your career growth and eventual job satisfaction.

CAREER WORK EXPERIENCE
PROGRAM OVERVIEW

Many students are undecided about their career goals and courses and need some knowledge, experience or investigation to help them make a career decision. Others wish to enter the work world for the first time but learn that it is often difficult to obtain employment without actual work experience. Still other students may be dissatisfied with their present job or career and wish to explore other options. These critically important needs can be met by the course CAREER WORK EXPERIENCE which helps students gain work experience, on-the-job training and exploration of a work environment by volunteering to work in a business or agency of their choice.

Students **attend** one class per week for 4 weeks. The class sessions focus on CAREER DEVELOPMENT. Topics include resume writing, interviewing skills, and job-search strategies.

Students **work** in a business or agency of their choice. This is done on a volunteer basis. Students **arrange** work experience time according to the number of semester credits they wish to earn. The actual work time is decided upon between the students and their supervisors. Students are evaluated by their supervisor both at midterm and at the end of the semester.

CAREER WORK EXPERIENCE COURSE OBJECTIVES

This program's primary objective is to enhance the student's career development. This is accomplished by giving students the opportunity to explore the world of work and receive experience and skills within local businesses and agencies.

Additional objectives are:

❑ To help students determine whether their aptitudes and interests are compatible with their educational and career goals.

❑ To enhance students' self-marketing skills.
    best qualified.

❑ To promote the setting of career goals.

❑ To demonstrate the vital relationship between college courses and the real work world through the concept of volunteerism.

CAREER WORK EXPERIENCE can be described as a *win-win* program. The students "win" as a result of their career growth. Cooperating businesses and agencies "win" because of the dedication, work and time donated to them by the students.

CAREER WORK EXPERIENCE COURSE REQUIREMENTS

The following are Career Work Experience course requirements. Students are expected to:

1. Attend the classroom portion of the course.

2. Choose a corporation, business or agency where they will volunteer a set number of hours weekly during the semester.

3. Select a work schedule that is satisfactory to both student and field work supervisor.

4. Turn in required assignments.

5. Keep careful records of field work attendance. Give duplicate field work attendance form to supervisor.

6. Turn in midterm evaluation half-way through the semester and a final evaluation at the semester's end.

7. Turn in signed attendance forms to complete and receive credit for the course.

8. Arrange several meetings with supervisor to evaluate student's work.

GUIDELINES AND SUGGESTIONS
FOR CWE STUDENTS

For the majority of you, this is the first time that you have been involved in an internship program. Therefore, I offer you the following guidelines and suggestions to help make your internship a pleasant, successful, and productive experience.

1. **TAKE CONTROL OF YOUR INTERNSHIP/WORK EXPERIENCE.** This control can be exhibited in a variety of ways:

   ❑ While selecting your worksite, it is important that you select the site that is consistent with your needs, goals and expectations. Do not go into it blindly. This is the initial form of control that you have over this experience.

   ❑ At midterm (half way through your work experience), you will be asked to sit down with your supervisor to formulate the 2nd half of your internship. At this time, both of you will reassess your responsibilities and take a look at additional challenges to be offered. At that time, you may want to present your supervisor with a list of goals that you would like to accomplish or achieve.

   ❑ Communicate (as much as possible) with your supervisor.

2. **ASK QUESTIONS!** Not only do questions assist you in obtaining information, but they have the potential to show motivation toward your work and worksite.

   Discuss and clarify when and where you will ask questions. Sometimes it is inappropriate to do so in certain circumstances, for example, when you are in front of a patient in the hospital, in front of a child within a classroom setting, etc. Generally, however, you are encouraged to ask questions.

3. **BE PATIENT!** Generally, the first part of your internship (2–3 weeks) will be somewhat observatory and information-gathering in nature, with less "hands-on" responsibilities. This is the "nature" of a typical internship. It takes time to acclimate you into a work environment, a company department, or the field in general. Your responsibilities and challenges will generally increase after this initial introductory period.

During those beginning weeks, get the most out of your experiences at your worksite. For example, if you've been asked to do a bit of filing, do it with a positive and learning attitude. You may be observing various procedures or situations. Put yourself in the other person's place and imagine <u>yourself</u> doing those procedures or dealing with the situation. Initially, alot can be learned by observing and this is often necessary in the beginning stages of an internship.

4. **BE CONSISTENT IN YOUR ATTENDANCE AT YOUR WORK-SITE.** Your regular attendance, or lack thereof, often reflects you as a person. If you miss quite a few days, are irregular in your attendance and/or are often late for work, you may not be considered responsible and your supervisor's attitude toward you may negatively reflect this. Conversely, if you are consistent in your attendance, motivated while at the worksite and are usually punctual, your supervisor most probably will be more positive in his/her attitude and actions toward you. If you have surgery or a crisis in your family, (something that is unavoidable), be sure to relate this to your supervisor. There are exceptions to the above if you communicate well with and are honest to him or her.

5. Ask for a "letter of recommendation" at the conclusion of your internship. This can be used in the future to assist you with your job-search efforts.

Good Luck!

SELF ASSESSMENT

The first step of career planning is to look inside yourself, exploring areas that have a strong influence on your career and life satisfaction. This self-assessment includes identifying your priorities, values, and skills you enjoy using.

PRIORITIES

According to Webster, a priority is based on "urgency, importance or merit." We all have priorities in our lives which we strive to attain or achieve. During career planning, it is important to identify your priorities, those things that are important to you and have the potential to contribute to your success and happiness within a career. What type of work environment do you prefer? What are the things that stimulate your energy and motivate you to do your best? Answering these questions will take you one step further toward achieving job satisfaction within a career of your choice.

VALUES AND MOTIVATORS

Why do some study for years for a career in engineering while others look for the easiest and shortest way to make a buck? What motivates a decision to change careers midlife after spending many years building an expertise and reputation within a particular field? The answer to both questions lie in your values and motivations. These are the forces that influence and guide the decisions you make throughout life.

If you value good health and physical fitness, you will be aware of good nutrition and, most probably, will incorporate an exercise program in your weekly routine. If you value career satisfaction, you should take time to examine personal values and make decisions consistent with them.

Values indicate what is most important to you in life. These self-motivators are reflected in what you actually do with your time. Personal values have an important influence on career decisions and, when translated into needs, have a direct relationship to job satisfaction.

You may discover you are dissatisfied with your present position or career because it contains few of your values and motivators. You may have settled for a job just for the money. Once aware of your values and how they motivate you, decisions can be based upon what is really important.

Do you value . . .

- ❑ Prestige and status?
- ❑ Influence over others?
- ❑ Opportunity to help others?
- ❑ Control of your work environment?
- ❑ Tangible results from your work?

When your life reflects your values, you will experience greater satisfaction and happiness within yourself and your work. When your life does not reflect your values, you may feel frustrated and dissatisfied.

SKILLS

If you were asked to list your skills, what would your list consist of? Since you are not accustomed to thinking and talking about your skills, it might be rather short. It may be difficult to recognize that you have a great variety of skills as a result of your life experiences.

Your skills include things you can do, your talents, and the personal qualities that you possess. You also developed skills by interacting with others, and going through your daily routine. Through assessment, you can identify those skills that you **enjoy** using, those that you have success with, and those that motivate you within a work situation or job. Your chances for job satisfaction will be greatly enhanced if you are able to use skills that you feel successful with and enjoy using.

INTERESTS AND PERSONALITY

Interest inventories ask you to indicate your likes and dislikes regarding a variety of tasks and subjects. The results give you an indication of the types of careers or fields that are compatible with your personality. Your interests are a reflection of your personality. Matching personality types with careers and work environments is based upon the following assumptions:

1. People are attracted to careers that give them the opportunity to express their personality.
2. People within the same career or field or work have similar personalities and tend to react to situations in a similar manner.

Your interests and personality will give you an indication if you will like working with things, ideas, people or data. Assessing your personality will move you closer toward choosing a career that will motivate and satisfy you.

It is important to note that your interests and personality will point you toward a number of careers that may have the potential to give you job satisfaction. This information, coupled with information on your values, priorities, motivators and skills you enjoy using will help you choose, among the many options, a career that will be both meaningful and satisfying.

The following exercises are designed to help you determine your career direction:

❑ *Exercise 1* gives you the opportunity to identify your priorities in relationship to a work environment.

❑ *Exercise 2* helps you to define those factors that motivate you to do your best in any given job or career.

❑ *Exericse 3* helps you determine values that will, subsequently, guide your career decisions.

❑ *Exercise 4* asks you to identify skills that you **enjoy** using, both on and off the job. Some skills are innate. They just seem to be part of you and your personality. Others take time to develop through training and practice.

EXERCISE 1

ENVIRONMENTAL PRIORITIES

Our work environment plays a very important role in our job satisfaction (or dissatisfaction). What type of work environment would you like to work in? The following is a list that relates different types or aspects of work environments. Add your own environmental factors to this list and relate on lines 1 through 10, those things that you would like to have as a part of YOUR work environment. **Do not** think of a specific job or career.

- Office
- Out-of doors
- Hurried, busy atmosphere
- Chance for advancement
- Few people
- Many people
- Large company
- Small company
- Plush, nicely decorated atmosphere
- Calm, low pressured

- Team-oriented atmosphere
- Competitive atmosphere
- Secretary or other people to whom you delegate work

- co workers
- back-up person
- customer service
- Safe from Hazards
- _____

1. Office
2. many people
3. Large company
4. team-oriented
5. Great Customer Service

6. team-oriented
7. back-up
8. Secretary
9. clean + nicely decor.
10. Safe from hazards

Using the words or phrases on lines 1 through 10, write a paragraph that describes your ideal work environment.

MY IDEAL WORK ENVIRONMENT

I would like to work for a large corporation in a team oriented atmosphere. I want to provide great customer service to our fellow employees and visitors. I would like to work with many people.

(turn to next page)

I would like to work in a clean and well organized office safe from hazards. I would like to have an assistant that I could delegate work too and to use as a back-up when I am out of office.

EXERCISE 2

MOTIVATORS

Rank these career and job motivators as to their importance to you.

	Least				Most
	1	2	3	4	5
Managing others as a part of my job			✓		
Size of company I am associated with				✓	
Having job security					✓
Gaining an expertise at what I do					✓
Having a chance to make a great deal of money					✓
Traveling as a part of my job				✓	
Variety in my work					✓
Having a high level of responsibility					✓
Being highly visible (noticed, influential)				✓	
Chance to run my own show			✓		
Helping others					✓
Working primarily by myself			✓		
Working primarily with other people					✓
Putting in a minimum of overtime at work			✓		
Working in pleasant physical surroundings					✓
Being involved in challenging work					✓
Other (list)_____					
_____					
_____					
_____					

EXERCISE 3

VALUES

Put a check by those values that are important to you.

✓   1. Prestige and status, including a great deal of respect from others.

✓   2. Opportunity to help other people or assisting others through my work.

✓   3. Job security, having a steady job which I am unlikely to lose. (To some, job security may also mean a steady paycheck, with no reliance on commissioned sales.)

✓   4. Opportunity to do new and different things, avoiding repetitious work.

✓   5. Opportunity for advancement.

✓   6. Control of my work environment, control of what I do and where.

✓   7. Seeing tangible results from my work.

      8. Working independently of others, being my own boss, doing the job the way I want it done with no one watching over me.

✓   9. Recognition, high achievement. Doing things of importance. Succeeding in a job that is considered to be difficult.

✓   10. Adventure, excitement.

✓   11. Flexibility of work hours.

     12. Physical activity, work that calls for moving around and using my physical strength.

✓   13. Creativity, being in a job that allows for the use of my imagination or generation of ideas.

     14. Routine work, uncomplicated work with the same tasks repeated often.

✓   15. Intellectual stimulation, allowing for the use of my mind.

     16. Close supervision, working under the direction of others, being told what to do.

✓   17. Distant supervision on the job.

     18. Economic prosperity, being well paid for your work.

     19. Leadership, influence over others, being responsible for and directing the work of others, making decisions that affect others.

EXERCISE 4

SKILLS

Circle the skills you ENJOY using. Include those skills that you have used very little but enjoyed using when you had the opportunity. Do not circle those skills you frequently use but do not enjoy.

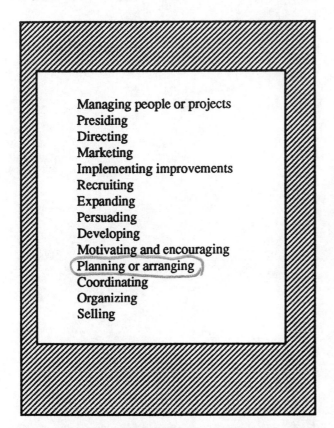

Managing people or projects
Presiding
Directing
Marketing
Implementing improvements
Recruiting
Expanding
Persuading
Developing
Motivating and encouraging
Planning or arranging
Coordinating
Organizing
Selling

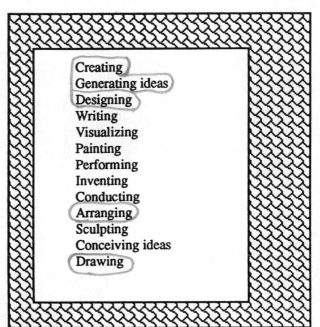

Creating
Generating ideas
Designing
Writing
Visualizing
Painting
Performing
Inventing
Conducting
Arranging
Sculpting
Conceiving ideas
Drawing

Enjoy and/or skilled at building
    or constructing
Skilled with or enjoys using tools
Skilled with hands
Highly dexterous
Physically coordinated and agile
Mechanical trouble shooters
Likes and/or skilled at repairing
    and adjusting
Inventive
Technically oriented
Skilled at doing crafts
Likes operating machinery
Persistent

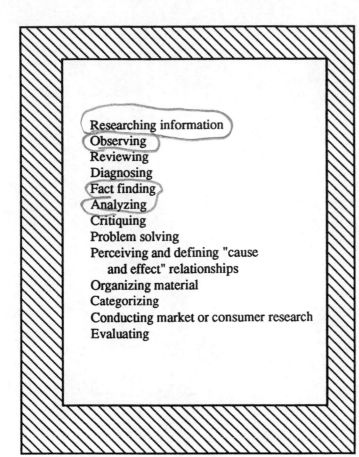

Researching information
Observing
Reviewing
Diagnosing
Fact finding
Analyzing
Critiquing
Problem solving
Perceiving and defining "cause
    and effect" relationships
Organizing material
Categorizing
Conducting market or consumer research
Evaluating

Listening
Relating well in dealing with
    public/people
Perceptive in human relations
Harmonizing
Sensitivity to others
Negotiating
Training or teaching
Supervising
Motivating
Giving feedback
Group facilitating
Fluency with words
Serving others
Supporting, encouraging others

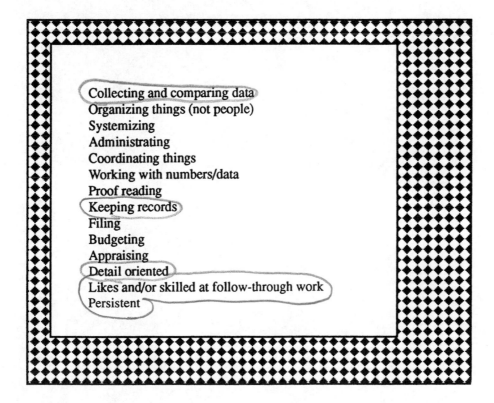

Collecting and comparing data
Organizing things (not people)
Systemizing
Administrating
Coordinating things
Working with numbers/data
Proof reading
Keeping records
Filing
Budgeting
Appraising
Detail oriented
Likes and/or skilled at follow-through work
Persistent

CAREER CLUSTERS

____ Sales Representative
____ Financial Analyst
____ Marketing Representative/Manager
____ Editor
____ Academic Dean
____ Insurance Agent
____ Principal or Educational Administrator
____ Stocks and Bonds Salesperson
✓ Personnel or Human Resources
      Specialist/Manager
____ Government Officer or Politician
____ Television Producer
____ Financial Operations Controller
____ Hotel Manager
____ Travel Agent
____ Industrial Engineer (EIR)
____ Receptionist

____ Controller
____ Sports Promoter
____ Lawyer
____ Judge
____ Sales
____ Traffic Manager
____ Retail Merchandiser
____ Curator
____ Banker
____ Real Estate Sales/Developer
____ Buyer (Retail)
____ Hospital Administrator
____ Paralegal/Legal Assistant
____ International Trade Specialist
____ Purchasing/Materials Management
      Specialist
____ Environmental/Hygiene Specialist

____ Public Relations Specialist
____ Novelist
____ Editor
____ Photographer
____ Clothes Designer
____ Drama Teacher
____ Musician
____ Dancer
____ Newscaster
✓ Interior Designer
____ Cartoonist
____ Audiovisual Producer
✓ Graphics Designer
____ Illustrator
____ Art Teacher
____ Conductor
____ Jeweler
____ Sign Painter
____ Picture Framer
✓ Model
____ Newspaper Columnist
____ Interpreter/Translator
____ Reporter
____ Set Designer
____ Music Teacher
____ Technical Writer
✓ Advertising (creative side)
____ Architect
____ Commercial Artist
____ Landscape Designer
____ Technical Illustrator

____ Secretary/Clerical Worker
____ Bookkeeper
✓ Accountant
✓ Bank Teller
____ Word processor
____ Medical Records Technician
____ Computer Operator/Data Processor
____ Auditor
____ Claim Examiner/Adjuster
____ Ticket Agent
✓ Dispatcher
____ Credit Analyst
____ Hotel Manager/Assistant
____ File Clerk
____ Cosmetologist
____ Marketing Research Worker
____ Sales Clerk
____ Typist
____ Escrow Officer
✓ Bank Loan Officer
____ Appraiser
____ Business Teacher
____ Cashier
____ Library Assistant
____ Financial Analyst
____ Statistical Clerk
____ Court Reporter
____ Receptionist
____ Legal assistant/paralegal
____ Operations Manager (CE)

_____ Chemist
_____ Astronomer
_____ Local Area Network Admin.
_____ Marine Biologist
_____ Architect
_____ Physician
_____ Dietician
_____ Speech Pathologist/Therapist
_____ Construction Superintendent
_____ Drafter
_____ Psychiatrist
_____ Statistician
_____ Environmental Analyst
_____ Physicist
_____ Biologist
_____ Zoologist
_____ Veterinarian
__✓__ Criminologist
_____ Quality Control Technician
_____ Medical Lab Technician
_____ Respiratory Therapist
_____ Air Traffic Controller
_____ Building Inspector
_____ Actuary
_____ Systems Analyst
_____ Psychologist
_____ Geologist
_____ Sociologist
_____ Design Engineer
_____ Urban Planner
_____ Electrical Engineer
_____ Pharmacist
_____ Osteopath
_____ Dentist
_____ Technical Writer
_____ Economist
_____ Landscape architect
_____ Audiologist
_____ Radiologist
_____ Nurse
_____ Physical Therapist
_____ Programmer
_____ Mechanical Engineer
_____ Mining Engineer
_____ Industrial Engineer
_____ Aerospace Engineer
_____ Civil Engineer
_____ Biomedical Engineer

_____ Electronics Technician
_____ T.V./Radio Technician
_____ Police Officer
_____ Pilot
_____ Auto Mechanic
_____ Welder
_____ Truck Driver
_____ Shipping Clerk
_____ Emergency Medical Technician
_____ Appliance Repair Person
_____ Electronics Assembler
_____ Quality Control Worker
_____ Computer Service Technician
_____ Machinist
_____ Air Conditioning Installer
_____ Butcher
_____ Painter
_____ Large Equipment Operator
_____ Landscape Gardener
_____ Forest Ranger
__✓__ Farmer
__✓__ Detective
_____ Fire Chief
_____ Ambulance Driver
_____ Mining Engineer
_____ Industrial Arts Teacher
_____ Radio Operator
_____ Mechanical Engineer
_____ Civil Engineer
_____ Aircraft Mechanic
_____ Fish & Wildlife Manager
_____ Surveyor
_____ Drafter
_____ Electrician
_____ Construction Estimator
_____ Carpenter
_____ Construction Worker
_____ Dental Lab Technician
_____ Biomedical Technician
_____ Manufacturing Technician
_____ Industrial Technician
_____ Semi-conductor Manager
_____ Veterinarian (RI)

_____ Flight Attendant
_____ Recreation Worker
_____ Waiter/Waitress
_____ Social Worker
_____ Minister
_____ Nurse
_____ Physical Therapist
_____ Dental Assistant
_____ Counselor
_____ Educational Administrator
_____ Health Service Administrator
_____ Respiratory Therapist
_____ Clinical Psychologist
_____ Radiologic Technologist
_____ Claims Adjuster

_____ Teacher
_____ Occupational Therapist
___✓___ Probation Officer
_____ Corporate Training Specialist
_____ Psychiatric Aide
_____ Librarian
_____ Employment Interviewer
_____ Community Dietician
_____ Career Counselor
_____ Speech Therapist
_____ Interpreter (deaf)
___✓___ Audiologist
___✓___ Loan Officer
_____ Medical Assistant
___✓___ Human Resources

___✓___ Human Resources (Personnel) Specialist
___✓___ Business Administrator
_____ Convalescent Hospital Administrator
_____ Educator
_____ Health Care Manager
_____ Insurance Agent
_____ Arbitrator (Labor Relations)
_____ Lawyer
_____ Manager
_____ Volunteer Administrator/Coordinator
_____ Advertising Specialist (A)
_____ Public Relations Specialist (A)

*Some Careers may be found in 2 areas.

INFORMATIONAL INTERVIEWS

One of the best ways to gain knowledge about an area of work or a career field is to talk to people involved in that career. Broadly defined, informational interviews consist of talking with another person for the sole purpose of gathering information about a particular field or career of interest.

More specifically, informational interviewing can benefit you in the following ways:

1. You can learn what is involved on a day to day basis beyond the understanding developed through your course work or gained from printed informational resources.

2. You receive the most current and updated information on a particular field.

3. You can get a perspective of the skills used in a particular position or job.

4. You have control of the interview. You can decide what questions to ask that will give you the desired information in your field of interest. This is possible because you are asking only for information, **not a job.**

5. You are gaining a network of contacts which may be helpful in the future.

How do I find people who will give an "informational interview"?

To find those people who are in your field of interest, consider the following:

❑ Who do you know in this field or job area?

❑ Ask friends, family, acquaintances (including professors) who they may know in your field of interest.

❑ Use the telephone directory to get the names of individuals or companies in your field.

❑ Find out the names of a professional organization in your field of interest and call an officer or member to gain information.

In most cases, these resources will lead you to people who can give you the desired information. It is recommended that you talk to a minimum of three people who are involved in a specific job or career field.

How do I arrange for an informational interview? What do I say?

1. Telephone the person directly or call a particular company within your field of interest. Ask for someone who is in the position to give you the desired information. Be prepared to explain that you are extremely interested in the field of _____ and that you are seeking information to help you make a career choice.

   Example: "My name is _____ and I am in the process of choosing a college major (or making a career change). Bob Jones, a mutual friend, suggested that I call you and indicated that you "might" be very helpful in helping me determine my career direction. Would it be possible for you to give me five (5) minutes of your time to answer some specific questions about your field? This information will be very important to me and will be very much appreciated.

   Most people will give you **more** than five minutes of their time, especially when they sense a strong interest and motivation. Some will offer to set an appointment time for an actual meeting. Take advantage of the opportunity to see their place of work, if at all possible. It gives you an added dimension about the field you are gaining information about.

2. You can choose to make contact through a letter and follow up with a phone call. Your letter would express your interest and desire for information.

Do not "drop in" with the hopes that you will be able to speak with either a particular individual or anyone available in your field.

What do I ask?

The following questions will assist you in gathering information about a particular career or job: (The questions that are bulleted will clarify a given career/job/position and help you understand how one might enter a particular career.

INFORMATIONAL INTERVIEW QUESTIONS

■ What is the nature of the work?

■ What do you do in an average day?

■ What is the range of your duties and responsibilities?

❑ What are the physical and psychological demands?

❑ Where is the work performed?

❑ What type of organizations employ people in this occupation?

❑ What are the working conditions?

❑ How does your work fit into the organization as a whole?

INFORMATIONAL INTERVIEW QUESTIONS—*CONTINUED*

- ❑ With whom do you work closely?

- ■ How did you get into this field and present position? *What did you have to do to get into the position*

- ■ What are the eligibility requirements for entry into the occupation?

- ■ What kinds of skills are required?

- ■ What kind of education is required?

- ■ What kind of specialized training is required?

- ❑ Are job opportunities in this field increasing, decreasing, or remaining stable?

- ❑ What are the projections about employment opportunities in geographic areas that you prefer?

- ❑ What opportunities are there for career mobility?

- ❑ Does this occupation offer you the opportunity to acquire skills and responsibilities that would allow you to advance in that organization?

- ■ What is the probable and potential earning power? At 5 years? At 10 years?

- ❑ What is the pay range and benefits (i.e., insurance, vacations, fringe benefits)?

- ❑ How rapidly do pay and benefits increase?

- ❑ Is there a maximum possible income?

- ■ What are the advantages and disadvantages of this career or position?

- ■ What advice would you give a person considering this occupation?

- ■ Where can I get further information? (Get several names if possible.)

EVALUATING THE INFORMATIONAL INTERVIEW

Make best use of the information you have received by asking yourself the following questions:

1. What did I learn from this interview? Consider both positive **and** negative information.

2. How does what I learned fit my personality, skills I enjoy using, values, motivators, priorities and goals?

3. What kinds of information do I still need to obtain in order to make a career decision?

ADDITIONAL INFORMATION AND GUIDELINES

❑ Send a thank you note to those who were willing to talk to you at any length. This is very important and considered a basic courtesy.

❑ If you ask for five minutes of a person's time, try to stick to that limit, unless it is obvious that your contact is amicable to spending more time with you. Respect their time!

❑ Seek a broad base of information. Do not do an informational interview with only one individual within a particular field. You can gain much information from the prospective of three or four individuals.

❑ Avoid forming an impression about a particular field based on the personality and like-ability of the person you have interviewed.

❑ An informational interview is **not** a job interview. Its sole purpose is to gather information to assist you in your career decisions.

SETTING CAREER GOALS

Goals can be vehicles that lead you toward accomplishments or things you want to attain in your life. They are something to work for and look forward to. They give order and direction to your life. Though they may change along the way, goals are energizing because they tell you what you can expect to accomplish. They can be thought of as road signs, telling you where you have been, where you are now, and where you should go next.

Setting goals increases your chances for success. Without goals to direct important educational and career decisions, you may find yourself in situations that are undesirable and for which you are not suited.

TYPES OF GOALS

You set all kinds of goals in life, some of which are conscious goals and some which are not. Consciously, you may set a goal to improve your grades or to complete a project by a specific time. Unconsciously, happiness and independence may be set as goals that you would like to achieve. These are called abstract goals.

Many of the goals you set are personal goals. Others relate to the world of work and are career goals. Webster defines a goal as "an end that one strives to attain." That "end," if sought in the far future, can be considered a LONG-TERM goal. INTERMEDIATE goals or OBJECTIVES are shorter term goals spanning over weeks or months and may lead to a particular long-term goal. Finally, each of the small steps you take to get closer to a larger goal can be defined as ACTION STEPS or MINI goals.

Example:

Long-term goal: To leave the field of accounting and become involved in another career.

Intermediate goals:

1. To investigate alternate careers to accounting. Target date: By May of this year.
2. To determine which career interests me the most and take steps to pursue it. Target date: By July of this year.

Action steps: (Specific actions that lead to accomplishment of your intermediate goals).

1. Visit the City Library career section for the next three weekends to research alternative careers for accounting. Check out any books that give me information. *Target date:* Completed by January.
2. Go to a local bookstore to purchase any books that may aid my investigation. *Target date:* Middle of February.
3. As a result of research, narrow alternatives down to three choices. *Target date:* End of March.
4. Talk to individuals who work in these three careers in which I am interested. *Target date:* Continuously through month of April.
5. If possible, visit people at their jobs. *Target date:* Middle of May.
6. Narrow down my alternatives to one choice. *Target date:* Middle of June.
7. Assess whether any additional education or training is necessary in order to pursue my new career. If so, take steps to pursue it. *Target date:* By July.
8. Update my resume. *Target date:* End of July.

In summary, your small ACTIONS STEPS help you to get closer to your INTERMEDIATE goals, which, in turn, help you to reach your ultimate or LONG-TERM GOALS. As the old adage states, *"a journey of a thousand miles begins with a single step."*

GOAL SETTING STEPS

The following goal setting steps will help you reach your long-term goal:

Step 1. Goal setting begins with the formulation of an *objective statement* that describes something you would like to achieve, have, or do. Is this goal realistic for you? Attainable?

Example: I want to be a physical therapist.

Do I like working with people? Do I like helping people? Am I strong enough physically to lift people? Do I like science? Do I get good enough grades to be accepted into a physical therapy educational program? Do I need instant results to be happy in a job or career? Or could I be satisfied with and accept delayed results? Is this goal realistic for me? Do I have the financial resources, time and motivation to attain it?

Step 2. Identify a strategy that will help you reach your goal. Develop INTERMEDIATE goals and ACTION STEPS as a part of this step-by-step plan.

Step 3. List *target dates* for the completion of each step. Target dates are important because they motivate you to accomplish a specific thing by a given time.

Step 4. It is important that your goal is *measurable*. Continuously check your progress.

Step 5. *Analyze* and *evaluate* your goals on a systematic basis and make necessary adjustments when necessary.

Identify possible *obstacles* that may get in the way of achieving your goals. Think about ways that you will overcome them.

Successful career planning involves defining your goals and knowing how to reach them. The more completely you plan out the steps along the way, the more likely you will be able to achieve your goals. The following exercise is designed to help you in the process of setting goals.

STUMBLING BLOCKS TO CAREER PLANNING

Many people suffer from stumbling blocks that hinder them in their career planning. Being aware of these blocks is the first step to either acceptance or working through them so that you can move ahead in the career planning process. The following are some of the more common stumbling blocks. Check the ones that fit for you.

❑ **Lack of Information.**
You do not have accurate information about the world of work. You do not know where or how to find information and/or are not attempting to find out. You are "spinning your wheels".

❑ **Fear.**
You have a fear of succeeding, making a mistake or making a wrong decision. You worry about appearing foolish.

❑ **Conflicts of Conscience.**
You are feeling conflict over the many roles in your life: Your role of being a parent vs. your professional career; your role within relationships vs. professional career. You feel guilt over your role responsibilities including childcare, your community responsibilities and your household responsibilities. You have a hard time spending time and energy on yourself.

❏ **Procrastination.**

You tend to put things off to the last minute and then feel alot of pressure. This pressure is tied in with fear and lack of time management.

❏ **Lack of Support System.**

You lack a good support system, people who can ease your responsibilities. You have a problem allowing others to help you and tend to always want to do it on your own.

❏ **Lack of Goals.**

You have not done any long-range planning. You don't have any career goals and, therefore, have nothing to reach or work for. You do not know how to set career goals.

❏ **No Time Management Skills.**

You lack good time management skills. You have a hard time prioritizing the importance of day-to-day tasks and long-range goals. You feel like there is not enough time.

❏ **Stress.**

You are feeling alot of stress and do not know how to deal with it. You are not looking at the causes of your stress and are not implementing a plan to help alleviate the pressure.

❏ **Difficulty in Making Decisions.**

You have a problem in making decisions. You have too many decisions to make. You are afraid of making the wrong one.

❏ **Desire to Conform to Society's View of What is Right.**

You do not recognize your uniqueness and tend to force yourself into a mold. You have a real difficult time trying to figure out what is right for who *you* are.

GOAL SETTING EXERCISE

Identify a five-year career goal, making sure that it is a realistic goal for you. Determine the intermediate objectives that you need to accomplish in order to move closer to your five-year career goal. Select target dates by which you would like to see your objectives completed.

CAREER GOAL (realistic, attainable, measurable)

complete "After Hours"

advance in my career

graduate MGC w/ Business Admin

INTERMEDIATE OBJECTIVES	TARGET DATE

GOAL SETTING EXERCISE—*continued*

List specific action steps you need to take to achieve the objectives. These steps should describe specific actions that will help you acquire the knowledge and information that is needed to achieve these objectives. List your target date for completion.

ACTION STEPS   **TARGET DATE**

_____   _____

_____   _____

_____   _____

_____   _____

_____   _____

_____   _____

_____   _____

_____   _____

_____   _____

_____   _____

_____   _____

_____   _____

_____   _____

_____   _____

_____   _____

_____   _____

OBSTACLES I MAY ENCOUNTER

_____

_____

_____

_____

_____

_____

_____

_____

HOW I WILL OVERCOME THEM (Activities or people)

_____

_____

_____

_____

_____

_____

_____

_____

_____

_____

_____

_____

3

JOB SEARCH STRATEGIES

There are very few subjects that are more vital to a person than the job search. However, few topics encompass more mystery. Nearly everyone experiences the task of searching for a job. People often enter this undertaking with a sense of frustration, dread, and uncertainty. The young, newly graduated student isn't the only one who is involved in job hunting. You could be searching for a job at any time due to lay off, illness or closure of a company. Great job security can be found in possessing the skills and knowledge to conduct a competent job search.

Searching for a job is hard work and can be very time consuming. Since no single method of job hunting works the best, it is beneficial to employ a variety of job hunting strategies to aid you in acquiring your target job or objective.

The following **job search strategies** will help you get to your target:

1. Prepare a *search strategy*. Set goals with a realistic timetable.

2. Put together a winning *resume* that best sells your education, experience, skills and accomplishments.

3. Make use of your *contacts. (Networking)* Job search experts tell us that about *80 to 85 percent* of all employment is gained through the job seeker's PERSONAL CONTACT NETWORK. A personal contact can refer you to a person who has a job to offer or give you valuable inside information about potential job openings. Parents, relatives, neighbors, alumni, present and former employers, teachers, members of professional organizations, service clubs, social groups, and members of labor unions and religious institutions can be all considered as personal contacts. (Be careful NOT to appear self-serving and interested in your own career and nothing else.) A personal contact network is like a mutual aid society; you help your contacts and they help you. Your contacts can give you advice and information within your career focus and can often open doors to a prospective job. People like to do favors for others. Allow them to help you. An expansion on the concept of "networking" is found at the end of this chapter.

4. Develop a prospect list. Make a list of 10–20 employers in the area who might be of interest to you. To help you do this, ask yourself "WHERE might I want to use my skills and education?" Pay attention to the ENVIRONMENT and your own VALUES. In what SECTOR of the world of work would you like to be involved?

5. Visit or join a *professional organization*. Here, you will have the chance to meet others in the career field you are entering. Ask your city librarian (main city branch) to direct you to a resource that gives the names of professional and trade organizations.

   The *Chamber of Commerce* is also a valuable resource for locating information on a specific professional organization that relates to your job target. Also, many individuals within your field will be able to give you the name of a related professional organization. Some organizations are a little costly. Try to go as "guest" or "visitor" for several meetings.

   Many professional organizations have a published "*job bank*," a list of job openings in the related field. (Professional and trade organizations develop clearinghouses and registers for their members, serving as an intermediary between job seekers and employers.)

6. Informational interviewing. Interviewing for information cannot only give you specific information on how to enter a field, but also can help you make valuable contacts within the field you are trying to enter. Talk to people who are in the job you want.

7. Library directories can often give you valuable information on what businesses and corporations are in your field of interest. The *Arizona High Tech Directory* will give you names of all of the "High Tech" companies in Arizona while the *Arizona Industrial Directory* will give you the names of manufacturers and distributors in all of Arizona. There are health care-related directories for those in the health care industry along with many other directories for a great variety of other fields. These directories can be found in the *main* library branches.

8. Use the *telephone directory* to help you develop a contact list.

9. Private *employment agencies* are a help when your skills are in demand. These agencies are often helpful for job seekers who have been working for a number of years.

10. Regularly scan the *business section* of the newspaper to receive information about new plants that are being built, companies that are hiring, new business ventures, etc. Also, the business section (as well as other sections) often contains articles that may imply a job opening without actually announcing it, such as the retirement of someone, promotions and resignations.

11. *Temporary agencies* can help you get your foot in the door. (This strategy is only helpful within certain career fields.) *Contract agencies* are a type of temporary agency allowing workers in various fields to work on a contract basis. This is quite common in the Computer and Engineering fields.

12. *Internships* provide a good opportunity to gain skills and experience and also recognition within a company or agency.

13. A small portion of jobs found are a result of the HELP WANTED ADS in the newspaper. However, do not rule it out as one of your strategies. Avoid "Catch Ads." They promise big money, easy working conditions, little or no qualifications, or short time involvement. They may use fancy titles such as "Executive position" or "public relations manager," and hide the fact that this position really could involve door-to-door selling. This type of ad sounds almost too good to be true, so you are tempted to respond and find out if it is really true. You may be required to buy the product that you will sell and you may end up stuck with it. NEVER sign on with a company that asks you to pay money first in order to get the job.

Example of "catch ad":

**A CAREER IN PUBLIC RELATIONS
AND ADVERTISING**

A well-known national company is seeking dynamic, enterprising people who desire the opportunity of earning up to $2500 per week. No experience needed. Will train the right individual. Must own dependable automobile. Call John Doe at 624-1234.

14. Women's centers can help women receive job leads and referrals.

15. College Placement Offices are an additional source of job leads.

16. Re-contact those employers who have said no previously. Sometimes, persistent, systematic re-contacts with the same person in each organization may lead to a job offer. (However, be careful not to do an overkill. You can call *too* often and become a bother to an employer.)

17. If you are conducting a *generalized* job search, meaning you are open to any location, a helpful resource in assisting your search is the *College Placement Annual*. It is an occupational directory of companies and positions customarily offered to college graduates. The *Annual will* assist you in locating companies within your major and geographic preference.

18. If you do not have direct contacts with a particular company or agency, apply directly to the Human Resources department. Try to get the name of the individual who does the staffing in your career field and address him/her in your cover letter. Some job seekers organize a "direct mail campaign" of letters and resumes to many organizations. Though this is not considered the best strategy, people have gotten jobs through this method. It is suggested that you follow up your resume with a phone call to the person indicated on your cover letter.

19. Send a resume to the manager of the department where you wish to work. Call the company to obtain that name. Many companies *will* divulge the name, however, some will not.

20. A *job fair* can give you instant access to a number of companies all at one time.

21. State employment agencies and their local branches offer a free job-finding service.

22. Many companies have a "hotline" that indicates open positions. Call the hotline once a week.

23. The internet is considered a "job bank" for job seekers. This strategy is more effective for more experienced workers.

24. Don't forget looking into city, state, or federal agencies. No one ever said that the job search was easy, but remember, all you are looking for is ONE job. If you persevere, you should find just what you are looking for. **GOOD LUCK!**

Be sure to send a thank you note after the interview. Use a computer if at all possible.

JOB-SEARCH TIPS

The following suggestions will assist you in your job search:

1. Assume that your job hunt will take months, not hours, days or weeks.

2. Expect more rejections than acceptances.

*3. Follow up every interview with a "thank you" letter. In addition to being courteous, you are getting your name in front of the individual who has the authority to hire you.

4. Think of your job search as a fulltime job. It takes time to write cover letters, send out resumes, call your networking contacts, follow up networking leads, interview, send thank you notes, make follow-up phone calls, in addition to utilizing many other strategies during your job search. Generally speaking, the amount of time you spend on your job search is commensurate with the time it will take to obtain it. (See "Factors That Affect the Timeliness of Obtaining a New Job/Position" on page 44.)

5. Don't worry every time you receive a rejection. Let that rejection spearhead an increase in your job search efforts. Rejections are inevitable. Your special job can be just around the next bend and can make itself known to you when you least expect it.

6. Taking a temporary job may not only help you with your finances but may also help to keep up your morale during an extended job search.

7. Be organized in your job search. Buy a special notebook to help in your planning, implementing and following through with appropriate job search strategies. Keep track of everyone you have sent resumes to or contacted by phone or in-person. You can never tell when you may need this information again. (See "Telephone/Personal Contact Form on page 43.)

8. Review your job search progress each week. Are you spending enough time on your search? Are you *waiting* for something to come to *you* instead of *you finding it?* What mistakes have you made? What is working? Are you using the networking process correctly? What else should you be doing?

9. Most job-search experts agree that an effective job-search campaign should involve as many strategies as possible. Are you using a variety of strategies in YOUR search? (See pages 34, 35, and 36.)

10. STAY WITH IT! A job hunt can be considered a numbers game that takes a great deal of time and effort. Tenacity and perseverance are your greatest assets!

HOW "NETWORKING" WORKS

As mentioned previously, studies show that approximately 80 to 85 percent of all employment is obtained through the job seeker's personal contact network. Each person that you know or may come in contact with may potentially have a job lead for you. Carefully plan your networking efforts by first making a list of everyone you know who could have contacts that could help you (See "Your List of Contacts" on page 41.) Unless you have just moved to a particular area, you will begin to realize the vast number of contacts that you have. Your list should be as broad as possible. (Your Accountant may not know of a job opening in your field but one of his/her clients might.) Anyone of your contacts may know of a job opening or a company that is hiring or may be able to refer you to someone else who does. The success of networking is based on a simple principle . . . that someone working for a particular company is likely to hear about any new positions that may be opening up.

Once you have developed your network, begin to contact them. Your goals should be as follows:

❑ Let your contacts know that you are looking for a job and would greatly appreciate their assistance.

❑ Briefly describe your education and related background.

❑ Ask them if they are aware of any present open positions or any positions that may be open in the future.

❑ In order to broaden your network, ask for names of other individuals who may be able to assist you. (Don't forget to ask if you can use his or her name when you call these individuals.)

By the time you have completed all of the calls on your list, your network will have greatly expanded. You will now be calling people you do not know but who could also bring you closer to a potential job opening. When calling these people, **do not** ask them for a job. Instead, ask for any advice that he or she could give you in addition to getting more names to add to your list. It is obvious that they will tell you about any job openings that they are aware of. Your goals are as follows:

❑ Introduce yourself and relate the name of the individual who suggested that you call.

❑ Give information about your field of interest, your qualifications, and ask for advice on how to approach a job search in this targeted industry.

❑ Determine if they know of any companies looking for someone with your education, skills and background. Additionally, ask if they could give you any names of any individuals who work within specific targeted companies.

NOTE: Your goal is NOT to ask for a job but to ask for ADVICE on your job search and to get names of those who might be able to assist you. People like to give advice and assist others who are out of work. Eventually, you will get to the contact who DOES know about the "perfect job opening for you"!

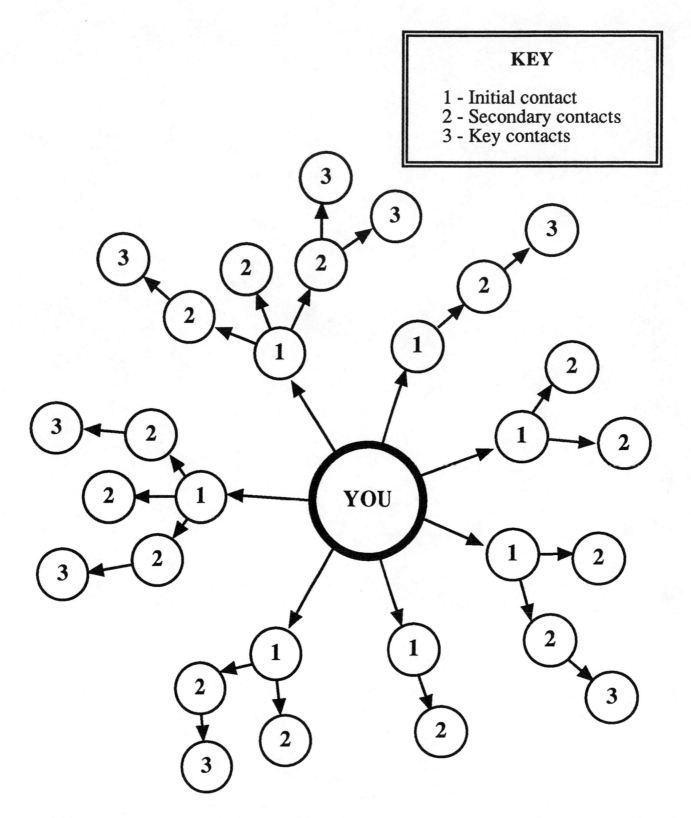

KEY

1 - Initial contact
2 - Secondary contacts
3 - Key contacts

YOU

NOTE: Your **initial** and **secondary contacts have the <u>potential</u>** to become your **key contacts**.

RULE OF THUMB: Before you leave a contact, try to get at least one name to further expand your network. **If you do not do this, you will "cut off" that "leg" of your network.**

YOUR LIST OF CONTACTS

WHOM DO I KNOW FROM. . . .

1. **My family?**

   ☐ mother/father
   ☐ sisters/brothers
   ☐ in-laws
   ☑ family friends *Pat + Julie B, Lynn*

2. **My children?**

   ☐ playmate's parents
   ☐ teachers
   ☐ coaches

3. **My old job?**

   ☐ former employers *James T.*
   ☑ fellow workers
   ☑ clients/customers/patients
   ☐ competitors
   ☐ vendors/suppliers

   Frank Jordan, Teresa L. Katrina C.

4. **My past?**

   ☐ friends/neighbors
   ☐ armed forces
   ☐ college friends, sorority/fraternity friends, alumni, teachers/professors

5. **Organizations/Public Service/charitable interest groups?**

   ☐ Chamber of Commerce
   ☐ volunteer organizations
   ☐ religious organizations

6. **My hobbies?**

   ☐ club members
   ☐ card groups
   ☐ sports groups (golf, tennis, bowling, baseball)
   ☐ athletic or exercise clubs

7. **Professional contacts?**

   ☐ lawyers
   ☐ consultants
   ☐ bankers
   ☐ politicians
   ☐ clergy
   ☐ dentists/doctors
   ☐ brokers
   ☑ owners of small businesses   Elen Malone, Tim Lloyd
   ☐ salesmen
   ☐ accountants
   ☐ insurance

8. **My file of business cards?**

9. **My Christmas card list?**

10. **My fraternal or social club directories?**

11. **Professional directories?**

12. **College alumni directories?**

TELEPHONE/PERSONAL CONTACT FORM

Contact's name and title	Company name and address	Telephone #
Frank Jordan Chief Police Service	Carl Vinson VAMC 1826 Veterans Blvd Dublin, Ga. 31021	478 212 510

Referred by:

Relationship: Co-worker

Objective of call:
- ❏ Networking or referral only
- ❏ Interview appointment
- ❏ General information
- ❏ Other _____

Script outline:

Goals: Ask yourself if these goals were accomplished before you left your contact. . . .

Did I accomplish the objective of my call?

Did I schedule an interview?

Did I obtain additional networking contact/names?
If so, who:

_____

_____

_____

Follow-up:
- ❏ Cover letter/resume sent
- ❏ Interview date and time
- ❏ Thank you note sent
- ❏ Contact additional referrals

_____

FACTORS THAT AFFECT THE TIMELINESS
OF OBTAINING A NEW JOB/POSITION

Each of the following factors will affect the amount of time it will take until you find your new job or position:

1. **LEVEL OF DETERMINATION**

   ❑ Are you conducting a serious job search? Are you diligent in your efforts, spending many hours per day in pursuit of a job/position?

2. **YOUR CONTACT BASE (AND THEIR VISIBILITY WITHIN THE INDUSTRY)**

   ❑ Do you have networking contacts within your field of interests? (Allow your contacts to lead you to others who may be able to assist you.)

3. **YOUR SALARY LEVEL**

   ❑ Is it realistic for the conditions of the job market today?

   ❑ Would you accept lower salary?

4. **YOUR SELLING POINTS**

   ❑ Do you have an area of specialization?

   ❑ Do you have any particular skills that are highly marketable?

   ❑ If you are looking outside your former field/industry, do you have specialized knowledge and strong transferable skills or contacts that will assist you in obtaining a position in a new industry or field?

5. **WILLINGNESS TO RELOCATE**

   ❑ Are you interested in obtaining a new position ONLY within your local area or are you broadening your possibilities with a willingness to relocate?

10 STEPS
LEADING TO EMPLOYMENT

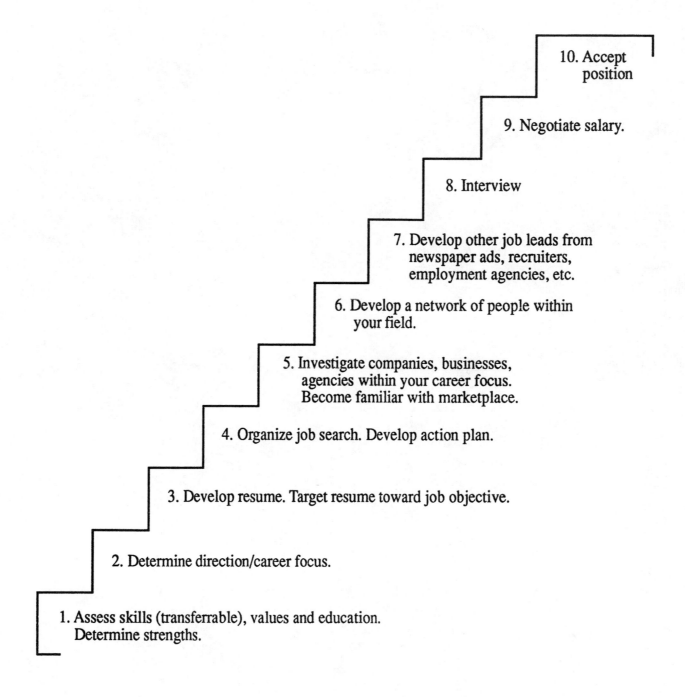

10. Accept position

9. Negotiate salary.

8. Interview

7. Develop other job leads from newspaper ads, recruiters, employment agencies, etc.

6. Develop a network of people within your field.

5. Investigate companies, businesses, agencies within your career focus. Become familiar with marketplace.

4. Organize job search. Develop action plan.

3. Develop resume. Target resume toward job objective.

2. Determine direction/career focus.

1. Assess skills (transferrable), values and education. Determine strengths.

4

THE COVER LETTER

Your *cover letter* is just one of the many steps you take in a job search. Its purpose is to introduce yourself to a prospective employer and focus attention onto your enclosed resume.

Address your cover letter to a specific person, not a department, company or title if at all possible. If you do not have a name, call the organization and request the name of the appropriate person to receive your letter. Libraries also have business and corporate directories in which names can be found.

Cover letters should be written on only one page and consist of three or four paragraphs. They are considered personal correspondence and should be hand typed or word processed. Mimeographed or photocopied mass cover letters are considered an insult.

Since this is a business letter, use high quality, 8 1/2 x 11 inch stationery. If possible, use the same stationery that your resume is printed on. This, plus a matching envelope, will present a very professional "marketing" package.

Your cover letter may constitute that first impression the employer will have of you. It is placed on top of a resume and comes before the interview. It should be neat, clean and technically correct.

Consider the following suggestions while composing your cover letter:

1. The **FIRST PARAGRAPH** should immediately capture the reader's attention. Indicate what position or type of work you are interested in and how you heard about it. (i.e., newspaper, mutual acquaintance, etc.) Use the name of a contact person, if you have one.

2. The **SECOND OR MIDDLE PARAGRAPH** should explain how your experience and background makes you a qualified candidate. Point out specific achievements or unique qualifications. Refer to the enclosed resume for details and highlight any specific skills or competencies that could be useful to their company. Your goal is to create enough interest so that they want to interview you. Be careful not to overuse the personal pronoun "I" in this section.

3. The **THIRD PARAGRAPH** expresses your desire for a personal interview and indicate your plans for follow up contact. Mention the enclosed resume.

4. Customize *every* letter. No generic letters should be sent out with your resume attached.

5. Use the same key words in your letter that appears in the job description or employment ad.

6. Remember good business letter-writing basics. Your letter should be brief, direct, polite, easy to read and understand. Do not ramble or place unrelated information in your cover letter. Ask someone else to proof-read your final copy.

In summary, these are the points to cover:

1. Reason for writing.
2. Statement of qualifications.
3. Reference to the company.
4. Request for an interview.

The following are only suggested formats for your cover letter. Create a letter that makes you feel comfortable and expresses your individuality.

SAMPLE COVER LETTER 1

2345 E. State Street
Seattle, Washington 91021

January 25, 2003

Mr. Joseph White
Transportation and Shipping Department
Westco Corporation
202 N. First Avenue
Phoenix, AZ 85013

Dear Mr. White,

I am interested in applying for the position of Transportation Manager currently available in your company. Several weeks ago, I talked to an individual named Joe Blanchard who indicated that an opening may exist within your department. Additionally, he felt that both my background and experience may be of interest to you.

I have had over eleven years experience as a transportation manager within the high tech electronics industry dealing with both a domestic and international customer base. During my tenure, I managed and directed the transportation operations of a multi-plant division of Star West, Inc., and directed over $2.5 million dollars of annual expenditures for divisional transportation operations.

My strengths include creative and innovative problem solving as illustrated by the development and implementation of a highly effective traffic departments operating structure for a rapidly expanding division. Additionally, I have extensive experience in the development of major cost reduction programs.

I am anxious for the opportunity to further discuss my qualifications for the position of Transportation Manager. My plans include being in the Phoenix area during the second and third week of January, and I would like to arrange to meet with you sometime within that time frame. I will call you next week to see if that possibility exists.

Sincerely,

Greg Jenson

Enclosure

434 West Brook Avenue
Phoenix, Arizona 85208
May 13, 2004

Mr. John Smith
Director of Personnel
Hillbrook Community Health Agency
P.O. Box 626
Phoenix, Arizona 85012

Dear Mr. Smith:

Your employment advertisement in Saturday's Arizona Republic for a Community Health Program Co-ordinator is of special interest to me. I feel that my education, skills and desire to work in community health make me a strong candidate for this position with your agency.

My education has given me broad exposure to the health care field and has also helped me develop sound analytical abilities. As a result of my involvement with the health care profession and various community organizations, I possess strong working knowledge of various private and public health institutions. As you can see from my resume, I have had extensive contact with patients and other health care professionals, all of which has contributed to my ability to communicate effectively with the health care community at large.

I believe that I offer your company a unique blend of community health-related skills. Additionally, I am a very enthusiastic and motivated individual and am often recognized for my strong coordination and communication skills. Thank you for your consideration.

Sincerely,

Jane S. Jones

Enclosure

5

WRITING A WINNING RESUME

A *resume* is a summary of factual information written about **you.** Your resume will introduce you to a potential employer and may result in getting you an interview. It also summarizes your qualifications for a job, indicates your job objective, gives information on past and present work experience, relates your education, and offers any other information that you may want an employer to know. Like an advertisement, the resume should attract attention, stimulate interest and encourage action. A resume can also be considered a marketing tool that allows you to promote yourself. A good resume will answer the following questions for the employer:

❑ What can this applicant do for me?
❑ Why should this applicant be considered for a specific job within my company?

Resumes allow you to tell about yourself in your own way. In contrast, application forms ask that you reveal yourself in specific terms designated by a particular company. Resumes give you the opportunity to capitalize on the skills and past experiences that have prepared you for the job you are seeking. Your resume is a ''snapshot'' of you.

Approach your resume like you would approach a basic marketing or sales plan. Your goal is to develop an effective method of selling your way into an interview. It is important to take into account your intended audience—the prospective employers. Ask yourself what skills and qualities is the employer looking for in a prospective employee.

BEFORE YOU BEGIN YOUR RESUME . . .

Before you begin to write your resume, you must have the answers to the following questions:

1. How do I let the employer know what type of position I am interested in?

2. What is a summary and how do I write it?

3. How do I treat my education?

4. How do I best indicate all of my experiences, responsibilities, skills and accomplishments that I have had as a result of past positions or jobs?

5. How do I treat my volunteer internship?

6. How do I indicate things about myself other than education and job history?

7. What *format* do I use? Chronological? Combination?

8. Once I decide on *what* I want to put in my resume, how should I actually put it down on paper? What should my resume look like? (Spacing, placement, etc.)

9. What do I do about references?

The following pages will assist you in answering the above questions.

GENERAL RESUME GUIDELINES

There is no one right way to write your resume, but there are guidelines you should follow.

1. Limit your resume to two pages or less. Few people will "wade through" a lengthy three or four page resume. There are exceptions to this rule, however. The education and psychology fields desire a more lengthy and detailed resume.

2. The top two-thirds of your resume is the most important. If the information contained within the first two-thirds is of interest to a potential employer, he/she will want to read on. Your goal is to attract the attention of the reader by putting your most "marketable" and important information first.

3. **Do not** include any personal information. No height, weight, sex, marital status, or health information should be included on today's resumes. Years ago, it was common and appropriate to include this information, but Equal Opportunity Legislation has changed what is acceptable for both resumes and interviews.

4. Hobbies should be included **only** if they clearly are related to career or job interests. Example: An individual that is applying for a position as a veterinarian's assistant could indicate the hobby of barrel racing. A computer analyst need not mention that his/her hobbies include skiing and tennis.

5. **Do not** use the pronouns "I," "me," or "my" in any of your statements.

6. **Do not** list employer's address. Only include name of company, city, state and title of position held.

7. Place your name, address, city, state, zip code and phone number at the top of your resume.

8. A resume is a **factual, historical** and **objective** account of your work experience. **Do not** include any **subjective** information in the **body** of your resume. Example: Do not say that you are "extremely responsible," "very dedicated" or "highly professional," even if you know you are. (If you choose to write a **summary** at the **beginning** of your resume, it is considered appropriate to include some **subjective** information, such as "excellent verbal and written communication skills," as long as it is true or factual.)

9. Your objective can be stated in either the cover letter or at the beginning of your resume. A cover letter should be included with all mailed resumes.

10. Use **action-oriented statements** when describing **skills, responsibilities** and **accomplishments.** Begin each statement with an action verb. Example: "established," "supervised," "advised," "analyzed," "assembled."

11. **Don't forget** to indicate your **accomplishments** and **successes** within past (and present) jobs. They often will set you apart from other applicants who are applying for the same position. Give information that shows you can **increase productivity, make or save money for your company, solve problems,** etc. If you can, **quantify** the **results** of your accomplishments in terms of **dollars, percentages** or **numbers.** Example: Implemented a new marketing program which resulted in a 25% increase in sales.

12. Use bold print and capital letters to emphasize certain points of information. (Use sparingly.)

13. **Do not** include references on your resume. Also, **do not** include a salary history or company addresses.

14. Prepare a resume that is neat and orderly. Space words so that there is enough white space, making your resume easy to read.

15. Give information that is factual, accurate and honest.

16. Indicate years worked, not months, if at all possible. Example: 1997–1998 instead of July, 1997 to December, 1998.

17. The ideal resume includes a few personal **qualities** (in the summary **ONLY**), **skills, knowledge, areas of expertise, accomplishments** and **results** that have taken place.

THE OBJECTIVE

Many resumes contain a career or job objective that is positioned directly under the name, address and phone number of the applicant. It is optional but is recommended in most circumstances. Many prospective employers flip through a stack of resumes, at first reading only the objectives. If they cannot determine what position you are interested in, they may ignore the resume. Therefore, it is important that your objective be as specific as possible. Don't waste time and space writing vague, wishy-washy objectives like the following:

- "To utilize my skills and experience within a position in a forward-thinking company that will allow me to grow in my career."

Your objective should be strong, focused and concise. The following objectives are considered appropriate on today's resumes:

- "An entry-level marketing position."

- "An Inside Sales position for an electronics company."

- "A position as Director of Career Services of a major college or university."

- "A position as an Electronics Technician."

- "A position on the Product Marketing Staff of a major manufacturing company."

If you do not put an objective on your resume, be sure to include it in the first paragraph of your cover letter.

THE SUMMARY

Today's resumes often include a summary statement that is written to attract the reader's attention. It should be a brief review of your background focusing on your expertise and skills, **but including only those which relate to your future job objective.** Properly written, a summary acts like a headline on a newspaper or magazine advertisement—it highlights the benefits you will offer and encourages the employer to read more. Summaries also have the potential to:

- ❑ Showcase areas of strong expertise that is relevant to the job you are seeking.
- ❑ Bring into the spotlight qualifications that may be buried in the body of your resume.
- ❑ Give you a way to emphasize the fact that you have many years of experience in a particular field, a fact that might not be immediately noticed if that experience spans over a number of jobs.

While your summary will be placed in the introductory (1st section) of your resume, write it last. Make sure that there are statements in your resume that verify what you have written in your summary. It is also appropriate to include any technical skills or qualifications that you may have. You may also use the title "SUMMARY OF QUALIFICATIONS."

SAMPLE SUMMARIES

1. **Experienced as** a public relations and advertising professional **with special skills in** media relations, corporate identity planning and print and broadcast advertising. **Highly competent in** crisis communications, issues management and positioning strategy.

2. **Over 5 years of experience** in the evaluation and diagnosis of automotive/mechanical problems. **Trained and experienced in** working on automotive transmissions and power trains, electrical and suspension systems, brakes, air conditioning, fuel systems and engines. **Recognized for** strong diagnostic and troubleshooting skills.

3. **Over twenty years of progressive** accounting **experience** with **broad expertise** in both public and private accounting environments. **Background includes significant accomplishments as** a CFO/Controller. **Possesses experience in** the real estate-related industry. **CPA certified. Highly competent in** multi-task responsibilities. **Particularly skilled in** the supervision of accounting staff. **A leader and team-player consistently recognized for** interpersonal effectiveness. Relies on strong technical and analytical skills to creatively solve problems while overseeing day-to-day operations. Combined skills, experience, knowledge, and strengths include: *(Include your list of skills, experience, knowledge, and strengths.)*

4. **Twenty years of combined experience** in management, Total Quality Management (TQM) and consulting in large and mid-size corporations. **Expertise includes** initiating, implementing and evaluating all phases of the TQM/Corporate re-engineering process. **Particularly skilled in** leading/facilitating large-scale process improvement projects. **Recognized for** building effective process improvement teams that are results/goal oriented. **Experienced** lecturer in the TQM process. **Additional skills include** management of professionals and technical staff, profit and loss accountability, strategic planning, technology assessment and implementation and project management. Strong commitment and drive as demonstrated by a history of promotions and an increasing scope of responsibility. Received TQM accreditation.

5. Senior level business executive with innovative management abilities and a **proven track record of** effective leadership. **Particularly skilled in** strategic planning, finance and general administration. **Recognized for** effective utilization of human resources and team building skills. A team player, dedicated to the accomplishment of corporate goals and objectives through vision, creativity and communication skills.

6. **Extensive background in** results-oriented management with emphasis on customer support/relations. **Experience in** the computer industry includes hardware and software support, project management, and provision of related services. Two years international experience. **Proven ability dealing with** commercial and political situations. Strong commitment and drive as demonstrated by history of promotions and increasing scope of responsibility.

7. **Extensive** operations and quality assurance management **experience in** high technology electronics through progressively responsible positions. **Background includes significant accomplishments in** overall plant management, implementing quality assurance improvement programs, managing products during offshore transition, and the development and installation of processes, equipment, and facilities to support new product and technology introduction. Strong team building skills have enabled the achievement of significant results utilizing MBO techniques and sound problem solving, communication and administrative skills.

SUMMARY
"BUZZ WORDS"

Today's resumes often contain a "**Summary**" or "**Summary of Qualifications**" statement that summarizes and emphasizes the candidate's strengths, skills, expertise and experience. It is suggested that you develop your summary last, after you have completed all sections of your resume. Use the following "BUZZ WORDS" to help develop your summary statement:

- ❑ Excellent organizational, verbal and written communication skills . . .
- ❑ Special emphasis in . . .
- ❑ Background includes significant accomplishments in . . .
- ❑ Expertise includes . . .
- ❑ Skilled in . . .
- ❑ Special skills include . . .
- ❑ Recognized ability in . . .
- ❑ Excels in . . .
- ❑ Effective problem solving skills . . .
- ❑ Highly skilled in . . .
- ❑ Over 15 years of experience in . . .
- ❑ Strong track record . . .
- ❑ Recognized for . . .
- ❑ Knowledgeable in . . .
- ❑ Knowledge and experience includes . . .
- ❑ Experienced as a . . .   (or experienced in . . .)
- ❑ Highly organized self-starter with _____ years experience in _____.
- ❑ Particularly skilled in . . .
- ❑ A team player . . .
- ❑ A _____ generalist . . .
- ❑ Trained in . . .
- ❑ Background includes experience and accomplishments in . . .
- ❑ Familiar with . . .
- ❑ Knowledge includes . . .
- ❑ Strong commitment and drive as demonstrated by a history of promotions and increasing scope of responsibility.
- ❑ Competent in . . .
- ❑ Acknowledged for . . .

There are three main types of resumes: *Chronological, functional* and *combination*. As the name indicates, the combination resume is a combination of both the chronological and functional resumes. A true functional resume gives no reference to dates or work history and only highlights the candidate's skills. It is recommended that you use either a chronological or chronological/functional "combination" resume format.

THE CHRONOLOGICAL RESUME

The *chronological* resume is the style of resume with which employers are most familiar. It is considered the traditional and most often used resume. Past and present positions are listed in chronological order, starting with the most recent first. Also included are dates of employment, companies and titles of positions held.

On the following page is a summary of the advantages and disadvantages of using a chronological resume:

THE CHRONOLOGICAL RESUME IS ADVANTAGEOUS

- ❏ when your job history shows growth.
- ❏ when the name of your last employer is an important consideration.
- ❏ when your career field has not changed. It is the same as that of prior positions.
- ❏ when your prior position titles are impressive.
- ❏ for the traditional fields of education and government.

THE CHRONOLOGICAL RESUME IS NOT ADVANTAGEOUS

- ❏ when you are changing careers.
- ❏ when you have a spotty work history.
- ❏ when you desire to de-emphasize your age.
- ❏ when you have no work history that relates to the position you are applying for or when you are looking for your first job.
- ❏ if you have been absent from the work force for a length of time.
- ❏ when your work history indicates that you have changed employers frequently.

THE CHRONOLOGICAL/FUNCTIONAL "COMBINATION" RESUME

A *combination* resume highlights skills and abilities of the candidate that **DIRECTLY RELATE** to the job objective or target. In this format, skills and abilities are emphasized first, followed by a listing of work history and education.

Listed below is a summary of the advantages and disadvantages of the "combination" resume:

THE COMBINATION RESUME IS ADVANTAGEOUS

- ❑ when you are changing careers.
- ❑ when you are entering the job market for the first time and have no work history.
- ❑ when your career growth in the past has not been good.
- ❑ when you want to emphasize competencies, capabilities or skills that have not been used in recent work experiences.
- ❑ when you are re-entering the "world of work" after an absence.
- ❑ if you have had a variety of relatively unconnected work experiences.
- ❑ when a large portion of your career history has been centered around consulting, freelance art or temporary work.

THE COMBINATION IS NOT ADVANTAGEOUS

- ❑ when you have had good consistent growth in your work record.
- ❑ when your recent employers have been very prestigious.
- ❑ when you have stayed in the same career field.
- ❑ for traditional fields such as government and education.

PREPARING THE CHRONOLOGICAL RESUME

By selecting the chronological format, you have chosen to highlight a good work history that has direct relationship to your present job target. You do not have large gaps or numerous career or job changes in your work history.

1. Start with your most recent position and work *backward.*

2. If you have a long work history, detail only the last four or five positions or employment that has covered the last ten or twelve years. An exception would exist if an early position was extremely relevant to the present position that the candidate is applying for.

3. Designate dates by using years. For example, use "1984–1988" instead of "December, 1984 to July, 1988".

4. Avoid repeating details that are common to several positions that you held.

5. Your education is not included in chronological order within the body of the resume. It is placed separately. You may want to highlight your education or place less emphasis on it.

6. Keep your objective or job target in mind as you describe past work positions and accomplishments. Place emphasis on those that relate most strongly to the position you are seeking.

PREPARING THE "COMBINATION" RESUME

You have chosen to highlight your skills and abilities rather than your past or present work record and to possibly play down any large gaps or inconsistencies in past work.

1. Select two, three or four functional skills or areas of expertise that you wish to highlight. They should **RELATE** either directly or indirectly to the job objective that you are interested in.

2. List them in order of importance to your present job objective.

3. Next to each skill or area of expertise, relate the most powerful experiences that you have had or things that you have done that prove you possess these skills or have these abilities.

4. Next, list places of employment, emphasizing those responsibilities that relate most directly to the job objective.

COMBINATION RESUME

SAMPLE LIST OF FUNCTIONAL SKILL OR EXPERTISE HEADINGS

Depending on your career direction and the qualifications you wish to highlight, your skill headings might include:

Accounting	Supervision	Programming
Promotions	Organization	Presentations
Investment	Architecture	Real Estate
Auditing	Program Development	Finance
Management/Managing	Counseling	Employment
Drafting	Medical/Clinical	Interviewing
Technical	Electronics	Chemistry
Graphic Design	Data Processing	Production
Printing	Computer Operations	Public Speaking
Layout	Communication	Fundraising
Marketing	Design	Community Affairs
Market Research	Engineering	Teaching
Construction	Planning	Product Development
Personnel	Scheduling	Testing
Advertising	Career Development	Inspecting
Secretarial	Instruction	Purchasing
Office Procedures	Social Work	Accounting
Administrative	Writing and Editing	Legal
Public Relations	Research	Physical Therapy
Culinary	Retailing	Customer Service
Aviation	Selling or Sales	Physical Therapy
Acquisition	Investigation	

. . . Plus any other word or words that describe skills that you have and wish to relate.

SUGGESTED HEADINGS FOR
RESUME SECTIONS

1. **For use when describing your education:**

   - ❏ Education
   - ❏ Educational Training
   - ❏ Educational Background
   - ❏ Area(s) of Competency

   - ❏ Competencies and Skills
   - ❏ Professional Training
   - ❏ Related Training
   - ❏ Technical Knowledge

2. **For use when describing your work experience:**

   - ❏ Work History
   - ❏ Work Background
   - ❏ Work Record

   - ❏ Employment History
   - ❏ Professional Experience
   - ❏ Professional History

3. **For use when describing your achievements or accomplishments:**

   - ❏ Selected Accomplishments
   - ❏ Professional Contributions
   - ❏ Professional Accomplishments

   - ❏ Personal Accomplishments
   - ❏ Outstanding Achievements

4. **Other section headings might include:**

   - ❏ Honors
   - ❏ Awards
   - ❏ Licenses

   - ❏ Volunteer Work Experience
   - ❏ Professional Affiliations
   - ❏ Certification

Samples of Education Formats
(for Resumes)

1. Degree Completed

A. Bachelor of Arts in Elementary Education, Arizona State University, Tempe, Arizona, 1993. G.P.A. 3.75.

B. Associate of Applied Science in Electronics Computer Technology, Glendale Community College, Glendale, Arizona, 1993.

C. Bachelor of Science in Electrical Engineering with a minor in Business, University of Arizona, Tucson, Arizona, 1992. G.P.A. 3.51.

2. Degree in Progress

A. Glendale Community College, Glendale, Arizona. Continuing education toward an Associate Degree in Accounting, 1990 to present.

B. Northern Arizona University, Flagstaff, Arizona. Continuing education toward a Bachelor of Science Degree in Marketing, 1991 to present.

3. Not Working on a Degree. Taking specific classes only

A. Glendale Community College, Glendale, Arizona. Specific coursework completed: Introduction to Microcomputer I and II, Microcomputer Usage and Applications, Lotus 1-2-3, (Level I and II), Database Management, WordPerfect, Microsoft Word.

B. Paradise Valley Community College, Phoenix, Arizona. Specific coursework completed:

- Introduction to Microcomputer I and II
- Microcomputer Usage and Applications
- Lotus 1-2-3, (Level I and II)
- WordPerfect
- Microsoft Word
- Database Management

62

RESUME ACTION STATEMENTS

The following are examples of **action-oriented resume statements** that describe **accomplishments** and **responsibilities** in a present or past position. Include percentages and numbers, if at all possible.

❏ Implemented a new marketing program which resulted in a 25% increase in sales.

❏ Coordinated and facilitated a set of workshops designed to enhance the career development of corporate employees.

❏ Designed a publicity campaign which resulted in company feature articles appearing in *The Wall Street Journal* and the *Businessman's Journal*.

RESUME ACTION WORDS

Use **action verbs** that imply motion, success, achievements, leadership, and responsibility to help you formulate **phrases** for your resume.

Accomplished	Coached	Diagnosed	Helped	Organized	Reported
Achieved	Collaborated	Directed	Hired	Originated	Represented
Acquired	Collected	Displayed	Identified	Oversaw	Researched
Acted	Communicated	Distributed	Illustrated	Painted	Resolved
Activated	Compared	Documented	Implemented	Participated	Restored
Adapted	Compiled	Drafted	Improved	Performed	Reviewed
Addressed	Completed	Drew	Increased	Planned	Revised
Adjusted	Composed	Earned	Influenced	Prepared	Revitalized
Administered	Computed	Edited	Informed	Presented	Saved
Advertised	Conceived	Eliminated	Initiated	Presided	Scheduled
Advised	Condensed	Engineered	Inspected	Printed	Screened
Allocated	Conducted	Enhanced	Installed	Problem-solved	Secured
Analyzed	Consolidated	Enlarged	Instructed	Processed	Selected
Applied	Constructed	Equipped	Interfaced	Procured	Served
Appointed	Consulted	Established	Interpreted	Produced	Sketched
Appraised	Contacted	Estimated	Interviewed	Programmed	Sold
Approved	Contracted	Evaluated	Invented	Promoted	Solved
Arranged	Contributed	Examined	Issued	Proposed	Staffed
Assembled	Controlled	Executed	Judged	Provided	Studied
Assessed	Converted	Exhibited	Launched	Publicized	Supervised
Assigned	Coordinated	Expanded	Located	Published	Supported
Assisted	Corroborated	Expedited	Maintained	Purchased	Surveyed
Attained	Counseled	Fabricated	Managed	Recommended	Taught
Attended	Created	Facilitated	Marketed	Reconciled	Tested
Audited	Decentralized	Financed	Mediated	Recorded	Tracked
Augmented	Decreased	Followed	Minimized	Recruited	Trained
Balanced	Delegated	Forecasted	Monitored	Redesigned	Translated
Budgeted	Delivered	Formulated	Motivated	Reduced	Typed
Built	Demonstrated	Founded	Negotiated	Reduced costs	Updated
Calculated	Designed	Gathered	Observed	Referred	Utilized
Clarified	Determined	Generated	Obtained	Regulated	Verified
Classified	Developed	Guided	Operated	Reorganized	Wrote
Cleaned	Devised	Headed	Ordered	Repaired	

ACCOMPLISHMENTS—RESULTS, RESPONSIBILITIES

In addition to relating your most important responsibilities, it is also very important to indicate your accomplishments and/or past contributions to the companies where you have worked. Use the following to assist you in determining accomplishments and results of your work:

Have I . . .

- ❑ Improved productivity . . .
- ❑ Recruited and trained . . .
- ❑ Lowered costs . . .
- ❑ Developed budgets . . .
- ❑ Organized and directed . . .
- ❑ Influenced the direction of . . .
- ❑ Influenced the efficiency and productivity of . . .
- ❑ Designed new forms . . .
- ❑ Evaluated performance . . .
- ❑ Minimized customer complaints . . .
- ❑ Improved product quality . . .
- ❑ Involved a team effort that produced . . . (what result?)
- ❑ Reduced labor costs . . .
- ❑ Designed and implemented . . .
- ❑ Increased market share . . .
- ❑ Reduced turnover . . .
- ❑ Reduced inventory . . .
- ❑ Increased sales . . .
- ❑ Improved cash availability . . .
- ❑ Reduced operating expenses . . .
- ❑ Planned and executed . . .
- ❑ Enhanced community relations . . .
- ❑ Developed (or revised) organizational plans . . .
- ❑ Negotiated settlements . . .
- ❑ Instituted cost controls . . .
- ❑ Helped others achieve their goals . . .
- ❑ Set new goals and objectives . . .
- ❑ Reduced billing cycle . . .
- ❑ Devised new strategies . . .
- ❑ Eliminated shipping errors . . .
- ❑ Set a record for . . .
- ❑ Planned and developed . . .
- ❑ Tested . . .
- ❑ Promoted from one job to another . . .
- ❑ Recognized with awards or commendations . . .

MOST COMMON RESUME WRITING MISTAKES

The following are the most common repeated mistakes that are found in resumes:

1. **Too long.** Preferred length is one page, however, two pages are acceptable.

2. **Hard to follow.** Resume is disorganized; information is scattered around page. Poor use of white space, indentations, capitalization, bold face type, larger type-size letters, and line spacing.

3. **Unprofessional.** Resume is poorly typewritten.

4. **Too sparse.** Resume gives too little information. Difficult to tell what you did and when.

5. **Technically incorrect.** Resume contains poor grammar, misspelled words and typographical errors. (Proofread resume before it is printed.)

6. **Doesn't tell what candidate accomplished while in past positions.** Your accomplishments (and results of those accomplishments) are important to note, as they have the potential to make you stand out above other applicants.

7. **Gives irrelevant personal information.** Candidate's height, weight, sex, marital status, and health information is not needed on today's resumes.

8. **Incorrect resume language.** Inconsistent tenses.

Check your resume to see if it contains any of the most commonly repeated mistakes.

APPEARANCE AND FINAL PRODUCT

LAYOUT

An effective layout is one in which the reader's eye moves quickly and easily down the page, focusing on key points or headings. To achieve this, a balance of typed words and white space (space without type) must be found.

The use of headings and subheadings enhance the readability and comprehension of your resume. You can emphasize information by using bold type, capital letters, underscoring, dots, dashes, or "bullets" to draw attention to important points.

ART

Do not use illustrations, unless you are writing an artistic or creative resume.

TYPE AND STYLE OF PAPER

A standard 8 1/2 x 11 inch size is suggested. The paper should be "bond" weight, or slightly heavier, and may have a light textured finish.

The color should be gray, ivory, white or off-white, *not* bright or offensive in color. (If you are writing a creative or artistic resume, some colors are considered acceptable.)

Cover letters and envelopes should be of the same stock, if possible. This gives your correspondence a more finished appearance.

Jill Annette Smith

2309 East Drayton Avenue
Phoenix, Arizona 85032
602-943-8998

OBJECTIVE

An Accounting or Bookkeeping position

SUMMARY

Over 10 years of experience within the accounting field with special skills in general ledger, financial statements and Accounts Receivable and Payable functions. Experienced in working with the accounting cycle from the recording of transactions to the preparation of financial statements. Knowledgeable in preparing and reporting cash flow projections, variances and statements. Strong commitment and drive as demonstrated by an increasing scope of responsibility. Combined experience, skills, strengths and knowledge includes:

- Quickbooks
- Excel
- Cash flow statements

- General ledger
- Accounts payable
- Accounts receivable

- 10-key by touch
- Journal entries
- Cash flow variances

PROFESSIONAL EXPERIENCE

2001-
2003
HEWITT AND ASSOCIATES, San Diego, California
Accountant for the Property Management Division

- Prepared journal entries and reconciled general ledger accounts on a monthly basis for three operating properties.
- Prepared monthly and quarterly financial stsatements.
- Compiled quarterly financial reporting packages that included information on cash flow projection, cash flow variances, balance sheets and monthly cash flow statement.
- Performed billing for over 500,000 rentable square feet of commercial office space.
- Performed accounts receivable/accounts payable functions that included invoice coding and issuing checks.
- Reconciled bank statements.

1997-
2001
BOULDER ATHLETIC CLUB, Boulder, Colorado
Controller (1999-2001)

- Served as part of upper level management.
- Supervised all functions, including staff, for accounting department.
- Managed cash flow and banking functions.
- Prepared monthly financial statements.

Payroll and Accounts Receivable Clerk (1997-1999)

- Processed payroll for 80+ employees.
- Computed and filed payroll taxes.
- Performed collection work to decrease bad debt.
- Processed all memberships and billing for a 4,000 member athletic club.

EDUCATION

Associate Degree in Accounting, Glendale, Community College,
Glendale, Arizona, 1997, GPA 3.85

Robert C. Smithson

120 West Ocotillo Road
Phoenix, Arizona 85012
602-265-1205

OBJECTIVE

To obtain a position in Operations Management or as an Assistant General Manager

SUMMARY OF QUALIFICATIONS

Over 20 years of experience in business and operations management. Background includes significant accomplishments in business growth, implementation of financial controls, reduction of expenses and labor costs, management of multiple facilities, strategic implementation of geographic commercial building sites and effective utilization of employee staff. Strengths in employee management and team building. Combined experience, skills, knowledge and strengths include:

- Day-to-day oversight of company/department operations
- Effective oversight of corporate resources
- Budgeting process
- Purchasing
- Identify/products/revenue streams
- Strategic planning
- Strong negotiating skills

- Profit/loss oversight
- Oversight of warehousing and transportation functions
- Management of employee benefit programs
- Accounts receivable
- Development of both internal and client-based marketing strategies
- Development of vendor contracts

- Mergers/acquisitions
- Coach/mentor/team building philosophy
- Advertising
- Event marketing/Direct marketing
- Sales promotions
- Conflict resolution
- Developed client-based external marketing strategies

PROFESSIONAL EXPERIENCE

1988-
2004

NATIONAL PRIDE, INC., Sioux Falls, South Dakota
General Manager
Responsible for managing a petroleum farm supply company with sales of $11 million and $2 million in fixed assets. Additionally, responsible to a 9-person Board of Directors for 35 employees, 7 branch locations and 3 leased facilities.
- Directed day-to-day operations including financial, marketing, warehousing and transportation, Human Resources and purchasing.
- Identified, recruited, hired and oversaw all department managers.
- Developed and implemented annual operating budget and strategic plans for company, including branch locations.
- Forecasted company's peak season product needs and negotiated forward contracts.
- Served as community representative, by representing various agricultural-related committees and organizations.

Accomplishments
- Developed the business from $5 million to $11 million in sales.
- Oversaw the $1 million renovation of main location that included extensive updating of equipment and new exterior.
- Built a regional 25,000 square foot truck shop for regional office.
- Oversaw the consolidation of the business through mergers and buyouts of existing companies to form present business.

1984-
1988

AGRI-REGIONAL COOPERATIVE, Minneapolis, Minnesota
Operations Manager/Assistant Manager
Responsible for the day-to-day operations of the petroleum division of a $9 million farm supply company.
- Managed the petroleum division for profitability and inventory controls for 3 locations.
- Assisted in the budgeting process, marketing, sales and distribution functions of the company.

- Established, implemented and oversaw a successful accounts receivable collection program for over $1.5 million in outstanding receivables.
- Oversaw the inventory of new supplies for petroleum, fertilizer and feed divisions.
- Managed the benefit programs for employees control system.

Accomplishments
- Cut the operating loan in half by successfully implementing a new accounts receivable program.
- Set up sales commission programs for employees.

1980- **LANDWAY COOPERATIVE, INC.**, Minneapolis, Minnesota
1984 **Sales Representative**
Responsible for the sales and marketing support of a regional petroleum company.
- Served as a sales representative to retail operations.
- Coordinated and conducted employee meetings to update and train on new products and programs.
- Called on prospective customers and on established accounts.
- Developed new accounts in both commercial and residential sectors.
- Presented information on products to existing and potential customers.
- Organized and implemented a perpetual inventory program.
- Supervised and trained inside sales staff.
- Facilitated meetings with local businesses in order to promote business and new products.
- Set up and attended trade shows.

EDUCATION

Minneapolis State College, Minneapolis, Minnesota

Susan Stone

901 West 70th Lane
Glendale, Arizona 85032
623-483-8871

OBJECTIVE

A position on the Product Marketing staff of a major manufacturing company

SUMMARY OF QUALIFICATIONS

Knowledgeable and experienced in using general marketing skills for the development of a product from concept to production. Excellent organizational, verbal and written communications skills developed while working on marketing, editing, journalism and financial staffs of major corporations/businesses. Won all 8 rounds of an educational marketing competition involving product, price, promotion and distribution variables for a fictitious software company. Combined experience, skills, strengths and knowledge include:

- Domestic markets
- International markets
- Product development
- Develop/implement telephone survey
- Market trend survey

- Competitive pricing analysis
- Computer skills include Microsoft Word, Microsoft Access, Quicken
- Very good presentation skills
- Excellent communication skills

EDUCATION

Master of Business Administration with an emphasis in Marketing
Arizona State University, Tempe, Arizona, 2003

Bachelor of Arts Degree with an emphasis in Psychology and Sociology
Akron University, Akron, Ohio, GPA 3.65, 2002

RELATED PROFESSIONAL EXPERIENCE

TRANSCOM CORPORATION, Phoenix, Arizona   2003
Marketing Intern

Served in an internship within the corporate marketing department as part of the product marketing team.
- Interviewed and collaborated with corporate departments in order to produce a new product.
- Interfaced and interviewed department managers in order to gain information and content accuracy for a redesigned and updated product.
- Conducted a secondary market analysis for the Network Services Division.
- Presented results of market analysis to management.
- Reviewed and edited the Network Services Division Sales Handbook.
- Developed a telephone survey to assess market trends.
- Created a sales tool that was designed to increase the profit margin.
- Designed and developed a student workbook for the Distributor Training Program.
- Redesigned and developed a sales program product that encouraged vertical distribution participation and provided information on services offered and order generation.

UNRELATED WORK HISTORY

BANK OF AMERICA, Tempe, Arizona
Loan Analyst

2000-
present

- Analyzes all loan applications and performs credit checks.
- Provides customer service to mortgage clients in order to resolve credit issues.

Business Women's Organization, Akron, Ohio
Intern

1999-
2000

- Increased advertising sales by soliciting ads from business members.
- Coordinated the entire production process.
- Set new goals and objectives for the staff and writers of a monthly newsletter.

HARRISON & LOMAS MORTGAGE, Akron, Ohio
Assistant to the Vice President of Loan Administration

1997-
1998

- Provided analysis of servicing efforts done by branch personnel.
- Audited foreclosure packages for adherence of government insured compliance requirements.
- Prepared initial litigation packages.

EDUCATIONAL ACCOMPLISHMENTS

Won all 8 rounds of an educational marketing competition involving product, price, promotion and distribution variables for a fictitious software company.

PROFESSIONAL AFFILIATIONS

Business Woman's Organization, Akron, Ohio, 1999-2000
Marketing Association, Phoenix, Arizona, 2002-2003

PERSONAL ACCOMPLISHMENTS

Ocotillo Yearbook Editor and Journalism Staff Member

ERIC T. ALLEN

2305 East Oregon Avenue
Phoenix, Arizona 85016
602-954-5938

OBJECTIVE

To obtain a sales position involving strong customer relations/customer service responsibilities while using prospecting and account development skills.

SUMMARY OF QUALIFICATIONS

Possesses extensive experience and accomplishments as a Field Sales Representative with an expertise in developing and maintaining exceptionally strong customer relations. Recognized for strong prospecting skills and the development of accounts. Skilled in analyzing competitive pricing, trends and developing sales strategies based upon market analysis. Participated in an exceptionally strong sales training program. Highly self-motivated and acknowledged for being a "self-starter". Recipient of numerous sales and contest awards. Combined skills, experience, knowledge and strengths include:

- Recognized as "Salesman of the Month". Nominated 21 times out of 22 months
- Need-based selling
- Competitive pricing analysis
- Prospecting for new clients
- Exceptionally strong prospecting/cold-calling skills
- Proposal writing
- "After sales" support

- Recognized for continuous sales increases
- Qualification of potential customers
- Creative approach to selling
- Training of new sales representatives
- Very effective in relationship-customer-oriented sales
- Strong presentation and promotion skills
- Strong negotiating/closing skills
- Promotional skills

PROFESSIONAL EXPERIENCE

1997-present   **KELLER OFFICE SOLUTIONS**, Scottsdale, Arizona
Regional Territory Sales Representative

- Manages sales in a protected territory (Tempe, Chandler, Mesa)
- Prospects/cold-calls on prospective customers.
- Provides excellent customer service to existing customers including customer training and "after sales" support.
- Prepares proposals and negotiates pricing.
- Trains new sales representatives.
- Creates and implements sales programs to enhance sales.
- Qualifies prospective customers and negotiates finance terms.

Accomplishments
- Chosen "Salesman of the Month" 5 times within the first 18 months.
- Nationally named as one of the "Top 10" Sales Representatives out of approximately 200 Manufacturer's Representatives.
- Achieved quota 21 times out of 22 months while averaging 140% of quota during those months.
- Promoted to Territory Representative after only 3 months of sales. Received an expanded product line as a result of promotion.
- Won a once-a-year sales contest out of 50 employees.
- Won certificate, cash bonuses and trips for sales achievements.

1995-1996   **CAMPUS INFORMATION ASSOCIATES**, Tucson, Arizona
Sales (Student Intern)

- Developed leads and sold advertisements for a campus "information/advertising system" within Arizona and California.

- Targeted businesses within and near various University communities.
- Developed leads and followed up with sales calls to potential customers.
- Made sales presentations that included determination of company needs and benefits of product.
- Performed "break-even" and "profit analysis" for each potential customer.
- Forecasted sales on a weekly basis.
- Quoted and negotiated pricing using a minimum standard base.
- Requested art work for clients, delivered to production company and placed finished ads within advertising space.
- Billed and collected monies from clients.

1993- **WEISS GUYS CAR WASH,** Tucson, Arizona
1995   **Sales/Assistant Marketing Director**

- Consistently achieved ranking as #1 salesman at Tucson location.
- Initiated and implemented a marketing research program designed to obtain information on the market position of the car wash.
- Determined research objectives and design.
- Designed questionnaire and sampling frame.
- Gathered, analyzed and interpreted data and developed a report that reflected research results.
- Trained sales employees in the use of appropriate sales techniques.

1991- **FARMERS INSURANCE**, Phoenix, Arizona
1993   **Telemarketer**
- Cold-called potential customers to gain information on present insurance status and to setup future appointments.

EDUCATION

Bachelor of Science in Business Administration with a major in Marketing
GPA in Marketing, 3.9
University of Arizona, Tucson, Arizona, May, 1997

HONORS AND AWARDS

Ranked in the "Top 10" out of approximately 200 sales representatives.
Salesman of the Month, 5 times
Dean's List with Distinction, (University of Arizona), Fall, Spring, 1996
"Intern of the Year", Finalist, Campus Information Associates, Spring and Fall, 1996
Vice President of Sigma Chi, Fraternal Organization, 1993-1994

Elaine D. Stafford, CPA

6437 North 80th Place
Phoenix, AZ 85020
(602) 487-6489

OBJECTIVE

To obtain a position as a Chief Financial Officer or Controller.

SUMMARY OF QUALIFICATIONS

Over twenty (20) years of progressive accounting experience with a broad expertise in both public and private accounting environments. Background includes significant accomplishments as a CFO/Controller. Possesses experience in the real estate-related industry. **CPA certified.** Particularly skilled in supervising accounting staff. A leader and team player consistently recognized for interpersonal effectiveness. Relies on strong technical and analytical skills to creatively solve problems while overseeing day-to-day operations. Combined skills, experience, knowledge, and strengths include:

- Strategic/Business Planning
- Budgeting Process
- Cash Flow Management
- Cost Reduction Strategies
- Insurance/Risk management
- Financing/Leasing
- Market Analysis
- Mergers/Acquisitions

- Financial Statements
- Accounting/Audits
- Staff Supervision
- Variance Analysis
- General Ledger, A/R, A/P, P/R
- Inventory Control
- Fixed Asset Management
- Benefits Programs

- Systems Development
- Telecommunications
- Computer Conversions
- Computer Skills include:
  Lotus 1-2-3 (Excel), Word,
  Internet, Windows 95/NT,
  QuickBooks, Real World,
  Peachtree, Unix

PROFESSIONAL HISTORY

2001-
2002
REMAX REALTY, Phoenix, Arizona
Controller/Director-MIS

Responsible for two major functions during the dissolution of Lyons Realty Arizona Company by Remax Realty. Major functions involved continued assumption of all controller responsibilities in addition to developing and implementing procedures to enhance smooth transfer of ownership.
- Supervised and led accounting staff through final year of accounting functions and corporate dissolution.
- Coordinated accounting functions between the two entities for consolidation of financial and statistical information.
- Interfaced with attorneys, public accountants, franchiser, creditors, and regulatory agencies to fully disclose change in ownership and prepared corresponding documentation.
- Executed all reports and summaries for new owner.
- Serviced as liaison between owner of company and new owner.
- Assessed and designed telecommunication networks involving multiple vendors resulting in increased efficiencies.

1995-
2001
LYONS REALTY, Glendale, Arizona
Chief Financial Officer (1996-2001); Controller (1995-1996)

Directed all accounting, financial, and reporting functions. Served as integral part of senior management and as a counsel to Board of Directors. Advised CEO and other administrative staff about all financial and accounting issues that related to the corporation.
- Developed and implemented strategic business plans with CEO.
- Obtained credit lines from local financial institution.
- Participated in development of and assumed CFO responsibility for ancillary services, i.e., Advantage

81

Mortgage Group and Fanin Insurance, Inc.
- Coordinated broker file requirements leading to reduction of E & O Claims, reduced legal costs and insurance savings of $40,000 a year.
- Assumed financial responsibility for acquisition process involving two real estate companies.
- Developed and managed MIS department while participating in implementation of company-wide computer training program.

1994 **JOHNS AND COMPANY,** San Diego, California
  Accountant
- Prepared monthly financial statements for 30 clients including compilations, account reconciliation and analysis, and related tax work.
- Handled accounts for many start-up entities and practices
- Prepared personal property tax returns.
- Performed additional accounting duties as overflow work from other departments including pre-litigation documents and fixed asset scheduling.

1988- **CONSULTING SERVICES/INDEPENDENT CONTRACTOR (Part-time),** Phoenix, Arizona
1994 **Accountant**
- Provided accounting services for eight corporations involved in land development, construction and property management.
- Acted as liaison with lending institution for construction and long-term financing.
- Prepared multi-departmental budgets.
- Compiled monthly financial statements and maintained general ledger for software development company.

1985- **LOGAN, FINLEY AND JONES,** Scottsdale, Arizona
1988 **Accounting Manager (1986-1988); Accountant (1985)**
- Managed accounting and reporting operations.
- Hired, supervised and evaluated accounting staff.

1982- **PART TIME EMPLOYMENT** (while in school)
1985 **Accountant**
- Provided accounting services for structural/civil engineering firm, food/salt brokerage, and retail/ wholesale operation.

EDUCATION

Certified Public Accountant, State of Arizona
Bachelor of Science, Business Administration, 1985, Arizona State University, Tempe, Arizona

PROFESSIONAL ORGANIZATIONS

American Institute of Certified Public Accountants
Arizona Society of Certified Public Accountants

Larry D. Smith

140 East Harding
Paradise Valley, AZ 85253

Home Phone: 480-988-1223
Cell: 602-763-2879

OBJECTIVE

Position as a Network/LAN Administrator or a PC/Network Technical Support Specialist

SUMMARY

Technical professional with comprehensive experience in computer hardware, software and data/voice networks. Excellent hardware and software troubleshooting skills. Knowledgeable in operating systems, server administration, installation and configuration of desktop/notebook computers, LAN/WAN configuration and help desk support.

TECHNICAL SKILLS

- TCP/IP, Telnet, DNS DHCP & WINS
- LAN/WAN design
- Router administration
- Ghost 7.0 & Sysprep
- Network analyzing tools
- Customer support
- VISIO
- A+; Net+; CCNA certifications

- Exchange Server and Outlook Enterprise Mail
- Windows 9x, NT, 2000, XP
- Network Administration
- Microsoft PowerPoint
- Microsoft Office 97/2000
- Sun Solaris UNIX 2.6
- Free BSD, SCO UNIX

- Compaq & Dell Desktop Notebook PCs
- MS Word, Excel, Access
- Network Integration
- Hardware/Software installation
- Terminal Services
- Hardware/Software testing

PROFESSIONAL EXPERIENCE

ARIZONA GAME AND FISH DEPARTMENT, Phoenix, Arizona   2002-present

Windows 2000 Network Administrator – Intern
- Performs account maintenance for users, groups and system services using Windows 2000 Server Microsoft Management Console.
- Maintains Windows 2000 Servers, manages user accounts and upgrades servers through OS service patches.
- Supports, configures and administers Windows 2000 servers in a LAN/WAN environment using TCP/IP connectivity.
- Troubleshoots MS Office, VISIO, HD file recovery, LAN port security and printer connectivity problems.
- Accomplishes Windows 9x/NT4 to Windows 2000 upgrades recovering all user information from old computers.
- Installs and configures Cisco hubs, switches, and routers with 56K to T1 speed WAN interfaces for local remote offices.

AG COMMUNICATIONS SYSTEMS, Phoenix, Arizona   2000-2002

Technical Service Engineer
- Installed, configured and supported Windows 9x/NT/2000 client computers, UNIX server computer systems, Lucent routers, Ethernet switches, hubs, Lucent firewalls, Lucent VOIP gateways.
- Installed and configured Windows 9x/NT/2000 operating systems and configured computers in a TXP/IP network.
- Installed and configured UNIX FreeBSD and UNIX SCO operating systems and configured computers in a TCP/IP network environment. Modified and wrote scripts accordingly for proper system operation.
- Configured, installed and supported Genesys Call Center server software applications on SUN enterprise servers as well as Genesys agent software on Windows 9x/NT/2000 Operating System desktop computers.
- Installed and configured Oracle relational databases onto SUN enterprise servers.
- Performed project management responsibilities including scheduling and tracking technical issues related to network integration.
- Analyzed and troubleshoot customer computers and network equipment and corrected problems found.

- Provided customer support over the phone and on site for all applications and hardware.
- Composed system as-built documentation and training materials and conducted customer training for all aspects of the customer network.

NATIONAL ACCESS, INC., Scottsdale, Arizona
1994-2000

Senior Applications Engineer (1998-2000)
- Performed system configuration, installation and maintenance of wireless local loop network equipment.
- Provided technical phone support for customer computer/network problems.
- Developed training materials and provided customer training on configuration, installation and maintenance of wireless local loop and CDX switching equipment.
- Installed, configured and supported National Access Compact Digital Exchange (CDX) class 5 central office telephone switches, Nortel PBXs and Comdial digital key telephone systems.

Applications Engineer (1994-1997)
- Conducted LAN/WAN design, installation, configuration and maintenance for customers.
- Provided 24/7 on-call support for all network devices.
- Provided systems engineering, installation and technical field support for voice/data/video wireless networks using digital 900MHz, 2.4 GHz, 18 GHz, 31 GHz and 38 GHz microwave radios.
- Conducted problem resolution using test equipment: BER testers, Spectrum Analyzers, Transmission Line Analyzers, multi-meters, oscilloscopes, etc.

GOLD STAR PRODUCTS COMPANY, LTD., Scottsdale, Arizona
1991-1994

Assistant Product Manager-Switching System/RF Products
- Coordinated development of digital telecommunication switching systems, cellular and cordless telephones.
- Authored product functional specifications detailing product hardware architecture, electrical specification and hardware/software capabilities and interaction in design of communications products.
- Performed and directed product evaluation and definition through hardware and software testing.
- Developed user guides, installation and programming manuals for all company products.
- Conducted competitive market researches and helped define product positioning in the market.

STI COMMUNICATIONS, Phoenix, Arizona
1989-1990

Telecommunications Technician

EDUCATION

Associate Degree in Electronic Computer Technology, ITT Technical Institute, 1988

CERTIFICATIONS

A+; Net+; CCNA
Telecommunications Equipment Grounding

ELAINE J. DAWSON

15228 N. Franklin Blvd, #1035 ◆ Scottsdale, AZ 85260 ◆ (602) 314-1891

OBJECTIVE

To obtain a part-time position as a speech and language clinician in an educational setting.

SUMMARY

Possesses extensive experience providing speech/language assessment and therapy to children from birth to five-years old. Highly competent in providing therapy in a variety of settings including one-on-one and group sessions within both special education and inclusive classrooms. Served as a member of a special education transdisciplinary team that assessed needs and provided services to children who qualified for early childhood special education programs. Services included treatment of children diagnosed with the following:

- Language delay and disorders
- Articulation disorders
- Phonological disorders
- Fluency disorders
- Voice disorders
- Hearing impaired

- Developmental delay
- Mild to moderate mentally impaired
- Severely mentally impaired
- Cerebral palsy
- Autism/pervasive development disorders
- Visually impaired

EDUCATION

Master of Science Degree, Communication Disorders, 1987
University of Wisconsin, Eau Claire, Wisconsin

Bachelor of Science Degree, Communication Disorders, Minor, Child Psychology, 1985
University of Minnesota, Minneapolis, Minnesota

CERTIFICATIONS

Applying for California Clinical and Rehabilitative Services Credential - Passed CBEST
(California Basic Educational Skills Test) as of 4/12/97

Certificate of Clinical Competence
American Speech Language - Hearing Association

Minnesota Teaching License - Pre-K-12
Educational Speech/Language Pathologist

PROFESSIONAL EXPERIENCE

1991 -   EDUCATION CENTER, EDEN PRAIRIE SCHOOL DISTRICT, Eden Prairie, Minnesota

1997   **Speech and Language Clinician, Early Childhood Special Education Program**

Responsible for providing speech and language therapy to birth through five-year olds with special needs. Services were delivered in a variety of settings including both one-on-one and group sessions, home visits, consultation to community day cares and pre-schools, and team teaching in both special education and inclusive classrooms.

- Developed and implemented a phonological curriculum for three to five-year olds with articulation needs.
- Teamed with other specialists to provide therapy using a transdisciplinary model.
- Assessed children, determined needs and wrote goals and objectives for individual education plans and individual family service plans.
- Participated annually in summer curriculum writing for phonological and inclusive pre-school classrooms.
- Provided in-service workshops on "fluency and speech and language development" to parents and daycare providers.
- Supervised student teachers from 1995-1997.
- Served as language curriculum representative.
- Served as "Building Union" representative, 1995-1997.
- Participated as a Multi-cultural Gender Fair Disability Awareness trainer.
- CPR certified.

1988 -   CARVER SCOTT COOPERATIVE, CENTRAL ELEMENTARY SCHOOL, AND

1991   WATERTOWN ELEMENTARY SCHOOL, Chaska, Minnesota

Speech and Language Clinician, Early Childhood, Special Education Program

Responsible for providing speech and language therapy to children two through five years of age in special education pre-school classrooms.

- Team-taught with an early childhood special education teacher.
- Provided services for children with cerebral palsy and developmental delay.
- Additionally provided individual therapy for children with speech and language delay.

1988 -   MINNEAPOLIS PUBLIC SHOOLS, Minneapolis, Minnesota

Summer   **Speech and Language Clinician**

- Provided speech and language services to autistic children from pre-school to high school.
- Provided therapy for high school population at various job sites in the community.

1988 -   MINNEAPOLIS PUBLIC SHOOLS, Minneapolis, Minnesota

Winter   **Speech and Language Clinician - Long term substitute position**

- Provided speech and language services to elementary age children.

BURNSVILLE SCHOOL DISTRICT, Burnsville, Minnesota

Teacher of the hearing impaired - Long term substitute position

- Provided services to school-age hearing impaired children at the elementary level. Itinerant position which required seeing students in different schools throughout the school district.

GRADUATE EXPERIENCE

1987 -   **HIGHLAND ELEMENTARY, ROSEMOUNT SCHOOL DISTRICT,** Rosemount, Minnesota

Fall   **Student Teaching - Speech and Language Clinician**

- Assisted with therapy and assessments.
- Acquired caseload and provided therapy for pre-school and elementary aged students in one-on-one and group settings.

1986 -   **UNIVERSITY OF WISCONSIN, GRADUATE PRACTICUM,** Eau Claire, Minnesota

1987   **Center for Communication Disorders**

- Provided speech and language therapy to children and adults.

Diagnostic Screening Clinic, University of Wisconsin

- Provided speech and language assessments to children and adults.
- Wrote assessment reports.

Development and Training Center, Eau Claire, Wisconsin

- Provided speech and language therapy for preschool children.
- Wrote and implemented lesson plans.

Hearing Clinic, University of Wisconsin

- Provided hearing testing with audiometer and tympanometer to children of all ages.

1985 -   **Y.W.C.A. DAYCARE,** Minneapolis, Minnesota

1986   **Head Teacher**

- Provided daycare for three month-old to five-year old children.
- Planned age-appropriate activities.
- Supervised assistant and substitute teachers.
- Promoted from assistant teacher to head teacher after six months of work.

PROFESSIONAL ORGANIZATION

Member of American Speech Language Hearing Association

CONTINUING EDUCATION/WORKSHOPS, (1993 - 1996)

"Learning Styles", by Eden Prairie School District

"Oral Motor Workshop", Facilitated by Suzanne Morris

"Peer Coaching", by Eden Prairie School District

Pervasive Development Disorders, St. Cloud State University

Sensory Integration For Disordered Children, Minneapolis Medical Center

"Team Building" Workshops, by Eden Prairie School District

"Pervasive Development Disorder/Autism" Workshop, by Eden Prairie Schools

JESSICA A. HOLMES
220 S. 4th St., #84 ◆ Phoenix, AZ 85022 ◆ (602) 938-2200

OBJECTIVE

To obtain a position teaching English-related classes within a secondary education environment.

SUMMARY

Knowledgeable and experienced in teaching English and English-related classes at the secondary education level. Experience includes teaching general writing, creative writing, computer-assisted writing and literature subjects. Highly recognized for developing and exhibiting a strong positive rapport with students. Additional skills/strengths include involvement with team sports (swimming/volleyball) that has resulted in the acquisition of numerous State and District Championships Awards/Titles. Received recognition/acknowledgment during student teaching experience for participation as a volunteer assistant for the swimming and speech and debate programs. Interested in continuing to utilize these skills within extracurricular sports education programs.

EDUCATION

Bachelor of Arts in Education with emphasis in Writing and American Literature
University of Wyoming, Laramie, Wyoming, 1996

TEACHING EXPERIENCE

**1996 -
1997**
ALBANY COUNTY SCHOOL DISTRICT #1, (Casper Junior and Senior High School), Casper, Wyoming

Substitute Teaching (English classes)

- Implemented lesson plans left by teacher.
- Guided English-related listening/reading activities, administered tests and assisted students with writing assignments.
- Supervised students in computer lab.

**1995
Fall**
ALBANY COUNTY SCHOOL DISTRICT #1, CASPER SENIOR HIGH SCHOOL (Grades 10-12), Casper, Wyoming

Student Teacher-English Classes (90-minute class sessions)

- Taught two Sophomore Composition classes in addition to one Humor and Satire Literature class and assisted with a class in Persuasive Speaking.
- Created lessons that accommodated a variety of learning styles.
- Organized daily classroom activities and implemented unit projects in literature, creative writing, and composition. Assigned, read, and commented on journal entries.
- Used the computer program called "Writer's Helper" as part of the editing process.
- Implemented a peer editing program in order to enhance students' writing skills.
- Volunteered as both a swimming coach and as an assistant for the Speech and Debate team.
- Implemented classroom management strategies utilizing a specific site-based program.
- Prepared students for the writing competency test throughout the semester. 100% of the students passed this test, a fact that was uncommon to the school.

1995
Spring   ALBANY COUNTY SCHOOL DISTRICT #1, Casper Junior and Senior High Schools, Casper, Wyoming

Practicum (Grades 7 - 12)

- Participated in and observed daily activities.
- Assisted teacher with grading assignments.
- Designed a lesson plan to assist students with vocabulary.
- Helped students on assignments. (4 weeks)

1994 -
Spring   ALBANY COUNTY SCHOOL DISTRICT #1, Casper Senior High School, Casper, Wyoming

Practicum (Grades 10 - 12)

- Observed students and teachers in a variety of classroom environments.
- Assisted teachers by helping students on various projects.
- Designed literature assignment for sophomore class. (4 weeks)

UNRELATED WORK HISTORY

1995 -   J.B.'S RESTAURANT, Casper, Wyoming

1996   **Waitress**

1992 -   UNIVERSITY OF WYOMING, STUDENT UNION FACILITIES, Laramie, Wyoming

1994   **Student Manager**

HONORS/AWARDS

College
University of Wyoming Swimming Team, Fall '90
Won various Racquetball Tournaments
President's Honor Roll, Spring '95
Dean's Honor Roll, Spring '94
Chosen as resident assistant, 1991 - 1992
Residence Halls Association, Spring '91

High School
Junior and Senior Class President
Student Council
Chosen to attend National Association of Student Council Conferences
All District Volleyball team
Captain of Volleyball team - Senior Year
Lettered in Varsity Swimming and Volleyball

PROFESSIONAL ORGANIZATIONS

Alpha Kappa Psi, Professional Business Fraternity
National Council of Teachers of English

KENNETH F. AHLER

2309 East 22nd Avenue
Glendale, AZ 85308

(602) 986-9126
Pager 486-0113

OBJECTIVE

An operations or manufacturing management position or a project management position with leadership responsibilities for assisting the organization to develop and sustain advantage in the marketplace through unique resources, agility, superior products and/or services.

SUMMARY

Over eight years of progressive engineering experience with a broad expertise in both a manufacturing and utility related environment. Particularly skilled in project management and plant/facility operation and maintenance. Competent in the development of project plans and schedules, the design, procurement, and installation of new equipment, and the supervision and coordination of plan execution. Excellent multi-task capability within challenging work environments. A team player consistently recognized for interpersonal effectiveness. Relies on strong technical and analytical skills to creatively solve problems. Experience and recently received MBA provide strong business sense and analytical techniques to provide quality products and services through strategic solutions. **MBA emphasis: Operations/Manufacturing Management.**

QUALIFYING SKILLS AND ACCOMPLISHMENTS

Mechanical Engineering Skills
- "Hands On" engineer with experience in working with pumps, turbines, motor, fans, valves, heat exchangers, HVAC controls and electrical control circuits.
- Experienced in facility/plant operation, maintenance and design.
- Personally contributed to the design, installation and commissioning of a $90 million plant system improvement project. As team leader of commissioning, implemented innovative testing methods to save time and budget.

Manufacturing Engineering Skills
- Evaluated cost reductions and redesign of problem areas to improve quality and simplify manufacturing.
- Designed circuit breaker component for cost reduction and manufacturing. Managed the components' development to the prototype stage.
- Evaluated motor per ANSI standards and conducted testing program to facilitate its procurement. Motor used in the first developed prototype of the circuit breaker.

Project Management Skills
- Managed multiple maintenance projects to completion including major equipment overhauls. These projects improved equipment performance, extended equipment life, thereby preventing unnecessary plant capital improvement costs. One project saved $253,000.
- Managed installation and commissioning of $1 million plant instrumentation project; installation and commissioning completed on schedule.

EXPERIENCE

COMED, Zion, Illinois

1991 to 1998

<u>Project Engineer</u> (1996 to 1998)
Responsible for providing engineering support to the operations of an electric utility, which includes managing multiple projects while interfacing with various in-house resources as well as outside contractors and consultants. Major projects supported the planning and execution of plant maintenance.

- Developed and implemented innovative cooling system allowing plant to continue operating at 100%.
- Performed numerous plant HVAC equipment improvements through successful design upgrade that resulted in increased equipment availability and reduced preventive maintenance requirements.

- Managed project plan, provided team leadership and training for all plant engineers as member of process improvement team. Responsible for implementing new master scheduling process. Final evaluation produced plans necessary for organizational change and implementation of the process.
- Managed multiple maintenance projects to completion including major equipment overhauls. That resulted in improved equipment performance, extended equipment life, thereby preventing unnecessary plant capital improvement costs. One project saved $253,000.
- Interfaced with regulators and recognized with commendations by senior management for professionally resolving compliance issues without further findings.
- Performed engineering analysis used to justify plant shutdown or plant continued operation.
- Promoted change to plant lubrication program, thus improving equipment lubrication methods and frequencies.
- Resolved personnel safety concerns by successfully soliciting bargaining unit and management opinions, communicating ideas, training, procedure changes, and plant design changes.

Mechanical Engineer (1991 to 1996)
Responsible for performance of assigned plant systems. Position required managing multiple projects while providing engineering leadership and expertise to maintain, operate and improve the reliability and performance of existing plant systems.

- Personally contributed to the design, installation and commissioning of a $90 million plant system improvement project. As team leader of commissioning, implemented innovative testing methods to save time and budget.
- Managed installation and commissioning of $1 million plant instrumentation project; installation and commissioning completed on schedule.
- Developed and made presentations to senior plant management requesting funds and maintenance support. The expanded budget and resources reduced the plant HVAC work order backlog by 50%.
- Administered and performed plant ventilation filter testing program per ANSI Standards which involved contracted technician and laboratory support. Contract provisions completed on time and under budget.
- Eliminated long-standing equipment problems through troubleshooting while utilizing strong mechanical/electrical aptitude.
- Influenced plant management to select an innovative solution, thus saving $330,000 in procurement cost alone.
- Organized and oversaw the timely replacement of a failed fan bearing which was threatening plant shutdown. Recognized with commendations in industry regulator's audit report.
- Performed root cause investigation of fan failures with the assistance of a failure prevention and investigation consultant. Corrective actions established prevented reoccurrence.
- Influenced the plant to use motor current analysis technology as predictive maintenance for large motors in order to extend time between overhauls.

SQUARE D COMPANY, Cedar Rapids, Iowa   1988 to 1989

Cooperative Education Engineer
While enrolled as a student at the University of Iowa, responsible for the redesign, testing and manufacturing support of molded case circuit breakers. Evaluation of cost reductions and redesign of problem areas to improve quality and simplify manufacturing.

- Designed circuit breaker component for cost reduction and manufacturing. Managed the components' development to the prototype stage.
- Evaluated motor per ANSI standards and conducted testing program to facilitate its procurement. Motor used in the first developed prototype of the circuit breaker.

EDUCATION

MBA, Operations/Manufacturing Management, GPA 3.7, DePaul University, Chicago, Illinois, 1998
BS, Mechanical Engineering, GPA 3.2, University of Iowa, Iowa City, Iowa, 1990

Richard K. Jones
1645 N. Mission Blvd
Gilbert, AZ   85233
(602) 857-8021

OBJECTIVE

To obtain a position as sales representative.

SUMMARY OF QUALIFICATIONS

Possesses extensive experience in sales-related training, management and the development of strong customer relations. Recognized for consistant growth in promoting commercial-based accounts. Highly energized/motivated self-starter. **Certified Sales Trainer.** Combined skills experience, knowledge and strengths include:

- Consistant double digit commercial sales increases
- Trained outside sales staff
- Oversight of inside and outside sales representatives
- Track sales and profitability of outside sales representatives
- Competitive pricing and trend analysis

- Creating/implementing strategic programs to increase sales
- Strong customer relationship skills
- Trade/home show organization
- Exceptionally strong motivation skills
- Negotiating skills
- Expertise in promotion of product

- Merchandising skills
- Inventory control
- Track profitability of store
- Manage day-to-day operations
- Team building
- Fiscal operations/budgeting
- Staffing/training employees
- Trouble shooting expertise
- Computer literate

QUALIFYING SKILLS AND ACCOMPLISHMENTS

Sales/Customer service
- Played a major role in positively affecting commercial sales volume at a rate of 40% over previous year.
- Interfaced with vendors for the purpose of developing programs to increase sales.
- Created and implemented strategies to increase sales and market share of company.
- **Certified as a trainer** in Forum Company's" Face-to Face Selling Skills" and "How to Manage Outside Sales Calls".
- Performed competitive pricing /trend analysis.

Promotions
- Recognized for organizing and winning a credit card sign-up promotion, collecting over **10,000 applications.**
- Strong track record for placing and winning departmental sales contests.
- Strong track record for both commercial and "do-it-yourself" customers.

Management
- Directly responsible with all aspects of managing a business including budgeting, forecasting, cost analysis, strategic planning and recruiting staff.
- Supervised daily operations of business.

PROFESSIONAL EXPERIENCE

**1997-
Present**

HOME DEPOT, PHOENIX, AZ
Store Manager

- Oversees inside/outside sales representatives.
- Tracks both sales and profitability of outside sales representatives.
- Manages both commercial and retail sales functions.
- Targets commercial customers with most potential for sales and margin growth.
- Interfaces with vendors to promote an increase in line of products and store volume.
- Trains outside sales representatives.
- Manages day-to-day operations of store, including hiring/training of staff, budgeting, fiscal operations and strategic planning.

GROUP STORE DIRECTOR (1997-1998)

- Oversaw all sales staff, both inside/outside and floor sales.
- Managed all day-today multi store operations and functions comprised of 150 employees and over $26 million sales volume.

1996-
1997

HENDERSON HOME IMPROVEMENT WAREHOUSE, HOUSTON, TEXAS
Store Manager

- Managed a retail store with an approximate sales volume of $35 million annually.
- Interfaced with store vendors to assist in the display and promotion of product.
- Tracked sales and profitability of margins.
- Performed budgeting, forecasting, cost analysis and recruiting staff functions.

1982-
1996

HOME DEPOT, Davenport, IA, Kansas
City, MO; Tucson, AZ, Phoenix, AZ, Mesa, AZ, Albuquerque, New Mexico
Group Store Director, Davenport, IA, (1994-1996)

- Directly responsible for a multi-store operation comprised of 180 employees and over $35 million in sales volume.
- Oversaw and trained inside/outside sales representatives.
- Interfaced and negotiated with vendors to secure product line and advertising funds.
- Organized and staffed industry trade show.
- Designed/developed advertisements for local newspaper.

Store Manager, Kansas City, MO (1990-1994)

Store Manager, Tucson, AZ (1987-1990)

Assistant Store Manager, Phoenix, AZ (1984-1987)

Store Supervisor, Mesa, AZ ; Albuquerque, NM (1982-1984)

EDUCATION

Bachelor of Science in Management, University of Arizona, Tucson, Arizona, 1982.

CERTIFICATION

Certified as a trainer for Forum Company's
"Face-to-Face Selling Skills"
and
"How to Manage Outside Sales Calls"
seminars.

ELAINE A. DAVIS

15228 N. Franklin Blvd, #1602 ◆ Scottsdale, AZ 85260 ◆ (602) 314-1501

OBJECTIVE

Seeking an Employment Recruiter position within a temporary, contract and/or permanent employment agency.

SUMMARY OF QUALIFICATIONS

Over 7 years of experience within a customer service environment. Highly skilled and experienced in both the initial screening and actual hiring process. Experience includes developing interviewing techniques, policies and procedures that were used by management. Additional experience includes performing as a liaison between hiring agencies and corporate department, creating staffing models and employee work schedules, and distribution of payroll.

QUALIFYING SKILLS

Interview/Selection Process
- Screened resumes to identify potential candidates for open positions.
- Served as a liaison between temporary agencies and Customer Service department to communicate requirements for specific job openings.
- Conducted telephone and in-person interviews for the selection of the most qualified applicants.
- Created staffing models and work schedules to meet department goals.
- Developed interviewing processes for specific department needs.

Payroll
- Responsible for activation of new employees within payroll system.
- Ran daily/weekly payroll reports. Verified individual time sheets for accuracy, made corrections and delivered reports to agency.

Customer Service
- Communicated hiring needs to agencies.
- Conducted "learning sessions" for temporary agencies, creating a more accurate understanding of the skills required for open positions.
- Assisted agencies with open houses during "hiring blitzes".

PROFESSIONAL EXPERIENCE

1994-
1996
SEGA OF AMERICA, Redwood City, California
Automated Call Distributor (ACD) Specialist (1995 - 1996)

Managed the telephone switch system. Responsible for interviewing and hiring of all temporary employees for department.

- Screened resumes from temporary agencies, interviewed applicants and selected most qualified candidates.
- Held 2 learning sessions for agencies to understand the requirements needed for our open positions.
- Developed staffing models designed to indicate department needs.
- Created new work schedules to meet high call volume

Consumer Service Supervisor (1994 - 1995)

Managed a group of up to 30+ temporary employees. Assisted with the interviewing and hiring of new employees. Performed payroll function.

- Participated in 3 open houses with temporary agency to recruit new hires.

- Contacted agency for termination of employees.

- Responsible for data entry of all new temporary employees into payroll system.

- Ran daily/weekly reports, individual time cards and summary reports. Verified reports for accuracy.

1991-   **INTEGRETEL, Santa Clara, California**
1994   **Inquiry Service Supervisor/Telecommunication Specialist**

Managed a group of 30+ representatives. Recruited and scheduled new employees. Developed performance standards to improve productivity. Assisted with the development of training programs and monitoring procedures to insure customer satisfaction.

- Worked directly with temporary agencies for the recruitment of new hires. Screened, interviewed and hired employees.

- Developed interview questions for specific job openings.

- Held bi-monthly orientations at temporary agency site in order to describe job descriptions and requirements to all interested applicants.

- Responsible for the scheduling of all new employees in order to meet call volume needs.

1988-   **US SPRINT, Burlingame, California**
1991   **Customer Service Supervisor (1989 - 1991)**

Managed a team of 14 representatives. Hired, trained, and appraised performance.

- Conducted telephone interviews to screen applicants.

- Interviewed qualified applicants and made recommendations to department manager.

- Motivated others to perform to the best of their abilities.

Customer Service Representative (1988 - 1989)

1987-   **COMMODITIES RESERVE CO., San Francisco, California**
1988   **Junior Account**

1986-   **MATTHEW BENDER AND CO., New York, New York**
1987   **Production Editor**

EDUCATION

Bachelor of Arts in Communications, December 1985
Purdue University, West Lafayette, Indiana

References available upon request.

CHRONOLOGICAL RESUME FORMAT WORKSHEET

Name __Kristin Denise Bryan__   Phone (478) 290-7147

Address __106 Poplar St.__
                      (number and street)

__Dexter__   __Ga__   __31021__
     (City)   (State)   (Zip Code)

OBJECTIVE   A concise statement identifying the type of work desired. Brief and very specific. Best if written with the job target in mind.

SUMMARY   A summary is used to highlight your best qualifications that relate to the objective.

PROFESSIONAL   List your jobs, starting with the most recent first. Briefly describe your responsibilities
EXPERIENCE   and accomplishments, using "action verbs". Related, more recent or longer term jobs will require longer descriptions. This will focus the reader's attention on your current marketable skills.

If you have been working longer than 10 years, weigh the importance of including the earlier jobs. If the skills/experiences have been covered in more recent jobs, these positions can be deleted.

Following each job description, highlight any achievements or successes you realized on the job. Be specific, using facts and figures to support your statement (i.e., increased sales by 150% within 2 years," or "designed, implemented a troubleshooting program which decreased downtime from 12% to 3%.")

111

1. Most recent job.

Carl Vinson VAMC   Dublin, Ga.
Company name   City, State

Job Title Security Asst.   Dates of employment July 08 - Present

Responsibilities, skills used, description of what you did on the job and achievements.

_____

_____

_____

_____

_____

_____

2. Next most recent job.

Carl Vinson VAMC   Dublin, Ga.
Company name   City, State

Job Title Retail Sales   Dates of employment 08/07 - 07/08
           Assoc.

Responsibilities, skills used, description of what you did on the job and achievements.

_____

_____

_____

_____

_____

_____

3. Job 3

Winn·Dixie, Inc.   Dublin, Ga
Company name   **City, State**

Job Title _Customer Servi_ Dates of employment _06|06 - 01|09_
            Lead

Responsibilities, skills used, description of what you did on the job and achievements.

_____

_____

_____

_____

_____

_____

4. Job 4

Dollar Tree   Dublin, Ga.
Company name   **City, State**

                                                    06|07 - 08|07
Job Title _Customer_   Dates of employment _04|06 - 04|07_
          Service Associate

Responsibilities, skills used, description of what you did on the job and achievements.

_____

_____

_____

_____

_____

_____

5. Job 5

Company name   City, State

Job Title _____ Dates of employment _____

Responsibilities, skills used, description of what you did on the job and achievements.

_____

_____

_____

_____

_____

6. Job 6

Company name   City, State

Job Title _____ Dates of employment _____

Responsibilities, skills used, description of what you did on the job and achievements.

_____

_____

_____

_____

_____

EDUCATION

List college degrees or focus you are pursuing in college. (**LIST HIGH SCHOOL ONLY IF RECENTLY GRADUATED—NO GRADE SCHOOL LISTED.**) For people with graduate degrees, include thesis or dissertation titles when applicable. Education should be placed either before work history or after it, depending on the amount of emphasis you wish to place on it.

WLHS _____ 05/2007

High School _____ Date Completed

Dublin, Ga

Location _____ Program

HGTC _____ 08/06 to 08/07

College _____ Dates

Dublin Ga _____ A+ cert.

Location _____ Degree

MGC _____ 05/10 to Present

College _____ Dates

Dublin Ga. _____ Buss. Admin

Location _____ Program

_____ to _____

College _____ Dates

_____

Location _____ Degree

OTHER TRAINING

List any specialized training or educational experiences not included above. (i.e., seminars, continuing education classes [if applicable], special projects, research posts, ect.)

- On the training Vetpro, background inv, owcp, + leave, + retirements, - completed 12wk course After Hours, - Powerpoint Excel training public speaking train.

PROFESSIONAL AFFILIATIONS

List organizations, societies, affiliations you are active in professionally. (i.e., ASTD, Association for Computing Machinery, American Society of Interior Designers, etc.)

R+R Goal Sharing
After Hours
Mentoring Buddy
controlled Substance Insp.
HR Collaborative
OWCP Task Force.

SPECIAL AWARDS/HONORS

List any professional or academic awards or honors you have received.

VOLUNTEER ACTIVITIES OR HOBBIES

Briefly describe any of your volunteer activities or hobbies only if they relate to your work on the job for which you are applying.

_____
_____
_____
_____
_____
_____

VOLUNTEER AFFILIATIONS

List any volunteer organizations to which you belong. List any boards or positions of note. (i.e., Kiwanis, Junior League, Lions, Soroptomists, etc.)

_____
_____
_____
_____
_____
_____

PROFESSIONAL LICENSES

List any professional certificates or licenses which are relevant to your work.

_____
_____
_____
_____
_____

PUBLICATIONS

List any publications, articles, etc., you have authored or co-authored.

Children's self-esteem
seminar article
_____
_____
_____

REFERENCES

Do not include references with your resume. You can state on your resume the words "References available upon request" or NOT refer to references at all. Either is appropriate.

"COMBINATION" FORMAT WORKSHEET

Objective

_____

_____

Summary

_____

_____

_____

_____

Qualifying Skills and Accomplishments

_____

- _____

- _____

- _____

- _____

_____

- _____

- _____

- _____

- _____

_____

- _____

- _____

- _____

- _____

WORK HISTORY

Job 1 (Most recent.)

_____

_____

Job 2

_____

_____

Job 3

_____

_____

Job 4

_____

_____

Job 5

_____

_____

EDUCATION

List college degrees or focus you are pursuing in college. (**LIST HIGH SCHOOL ONLY IF RECENTLY GRADUATED—NO GRADE SCHOOL LISTED.**) For people with graduate degrees, include thesis or dissertation titles when applicable. Education should be placed either before work history or after it, depending on the amount of emphasis you wish to place on it.

High School	Date Completed
Location	Program
	to
College	Dates
Location	Degree
	to
College	Dates
Location	Program
	to
College	Dates
Location	Degree

OTHER TRAINING

List any specialized training or educational experiences not included above. (i.e., seminars, continuing education classes [if applicable], special projects, research posts, etc.)

_____

_____

_____

_____

_____

_____

_____

_____

PROFESSIONAL AFFILIATIONS

List organizations, societies, affiliations you are active in professionally. (i.e., ASTD, Association for Computing Machinery, American Society of Interior Designers, etc.)

_____

_____

_____

_____

_____

_____

_____

_____

SPECIAL AWARDS/HONORS

List any professional or academic awards or honors you have received.

_____
_____
_____
_____
_____
_____

VOLUNTEER ACTIVITIES OR HOBBIES

Briefly describe any of your volunteer activities or hobbies only if they relate to your work on the job for which you are applying.

_____
_____
_____
_____
_____
_____
_____

VOLUNTEER AFFILIATIONS

List any volunteer organizations to which you belong. List any boards or positions of note. (i.e., Kiwanis, Junior League, Lions, Soroptomists, etc.)

_____
_____
_____
_____
_____
_____

PROFESSIONAL LICENSES

List any professional certificates or licenses which are relevant to your work.

_____
_____
_____
_____
_____

PUBLICATIONS

List any publications, articles, etc., you have authored or co-authored.

_____
_____
_____
_____
_____

REFERENCES

Do not include references with your resume. You can state on your resume the words "References available upon request" or NOT refer to references at all. Either is appropriate.

6

FILLING OUT APPLICATION FORMS

The *employment application* is a form used by many companies or organizations to gain necessary information on individuals seeking a position within their organization. Many times, the employer or interviewer wants to make rapid comparisons and uses his organization's employment application for that purpose. For example, Mr. White needed a data entry operator who could type fairly fast. By thumbing through many applications and referring to the same blank each time, he could quickly compare the candidates and, thus, eliminate all of those who had only an average speed.

Since your selection for an interview or job may depend on how you fill out an application, you should observe carefully the following guidelines:

1. Fill out the application neatly and accurately as possible, paying careful attention to correct spelling and punctuation. If it is possible, obtain several copies of the application from the business or agency where you are applying and TYPE in the necessary information. If handwritten, print in *black* ink. (Most organizations will send you several application forms if you call and request them.)

2. Never leave an item blank. If a question does not apply, write N/A (not applicable), showing that you did not overlook the question.

3. Be specific when asked for "job preference" or "position desired." DO NOT write "anything." It is important to state clearly the type of work or position you are seeking.

4. If you are filling out the application at the place of employment, take a prepared list of schools attended and employers. Include addresses, phone numbers, and dates of your attendance and/or employment.

5. You will be asked to list references. It is suggested that you ask permission of those you plan to list. References of most value to an employer are work-related references. Other references that are considered to be good are from a recognized community leader, a teacher who knows you well, or from friends who are established in business.

6. Never state a salary requirement on an application if you can possibly avoid it. Instead, type in or print the words *"open"* or *"negotiable"*. If you mention a price, chances are you are either overpricing yourself or underpricing yourself in the employer's mind. If a fixed salary rate is to be given, you will soon find out that fact. In summary, if you don't know the employer's mind on salary, it's much safer to answer this question with the words "open" or "negotiable."

7. Questions pertaining to your availability for work should be answered as liberally as possible. Do not list preferences for days and shifts unless you have very clear restrictions. If you would rather not work nights, but would for awhile if necessary to get the job, simply indicate that you are available for all shifts. Indicate that you could start "immediately" unless you are concurrently employed. If working, it is usually safe to enter the words "two week notice." This shows that you are considerate of your present employer and gives the impression you will be a considerate employee at this company or agency as well.

   "Part-time" usually means a permanent job that is less than 40 hours per week. "Temporary" usually means a full-time job, but only for a limited time until a *scheduled* lay off. It is advisable to indicate availability for these (if you are), because they often can lead into regular full-time permanent work.

8. Remember the rule to never put anything on the application form which will reduce your chances of being selected for an interview. Therefore, avoid words such as "fired," "quit for personal reasons," or even "terminated." You can (and probably must) explain in the interview, so on the application form use ambiguous but true terms such as "left," "released," "laid off," and "job ended," or "left to develop my career."

9. List your most recent jobs first.

MARICOPA COMMUNITY COLLEGES

EMPLOYMENT APPLICATION
MARICOPA COMMUNITY COLLEGES

Job Posting # _____

Input Operator _____

Human Resources Department
3910 E. Washington
Phoenix, Arizona 85034
(602) 267-4395

Name _____ Date _____
        Last Name   First Name   Middle Name

Address _____
      Street   City   State   Zip

Area Code & Telephone Number _____

Area Code & Message Number _____

Position Desired _____ Social Security Number _____

College/District Location _____

EMPLOYMENT HISTORY — This section must be completed. If you wish to elaborate, attach resume.
List 10 years previous work experience. (List most recent experience first)

Inclusive Dates From To	Name of Employer Name of Supervisor	Address of Employer	Title of Position & Description of Duties	Full or Part Time

May we contact the employers listed above? _____ All but current employer _____

Have you ever been convicted of a felony? _____ Availability Date _____

123

EDUCATION:

Circle Highest Grade Completed: 1 2 3 4 5 6 7 8 9 10 11 12 13 14 15 16 17 18 19 20

School	How Many Years	Name of School	Location	Major Subject	Did you graduate? (Degree, Year, Discipline)
High School/GED	✕				
College					
Graduate					
Other (Apprentice)					
Business or Vocational					
License #					

List office equipment/machines which you can operate proficiently _____

_____

Indicate wpm, if you: type _____   take shorthand _____

Please list any other qualifications that you feel would especially qualify you for this position.

_____

_____

EMPLOYMENT REFERENCES

Please list three supervisors you wish to give as references (**present or prior employers**).

Supervisors Full Name	Address/Telephone Number	Position You Held
1.		
2.		
3.		

PLEASE READ CAREFULLY: APPLICANT'S CERTIFICATION AND AGREEMENT

I hereby certify that the facts set forth in the above employment application are true and complete to the best of my knowledge. I understand that falsified statements on this application shall be considered sufficient cause for rejection of this application or dismissal. As conditions of employment, I also understand that if I am extended a job offer, I will be required to provide original and/or certified documents for work authorization and identity to prove that I am authorized to work in the United States per the "Immigration Reform and Control Act of 1986".

Date: _____   _____

Signature of Applicant

HOW TO MARKET YOURSELF:
Interviews

Will Rogers first said it: "You never get a second chance to make a good first impression." An interview is, most of all, an opportunity. But to take advantage of such an opportunity, you need to approach it confidently and with enthusiasm. Understanding a few things about interviews beforehand will help you build both confidence and enthusiasm. In this section, you will be given information and guidelines toward positive and successful interviewing.

INTERVIEW PREPARATION

When planning for a job interview, be prepared to SELL YOURSELF. No matter what type of interview you experience, most questions are asked to determine the following information:

1. How can this person help me/my organization?

2. Will she/he fit in our organization?

3. Why does this person want to work for this organization?

4. What will it cost to employ this individual?

Your goal during your job interview is to be able to answer these questions for the interviewer. It is important to place your focus on how YOU can meet THEIR needs.

BEFORE THE INTERVIEW

Learn as much as you can about the company or organization. The following is a sample of questions you should be informed about prior to the first interview:

1. What are the company's primary products or services?

2. What is the size of this company? What growth rate have they experienced in the last five years? What future growth are they planning in the next five years?

3. What is this organization's reputation in the community? In the field?

4. Who are their major customers?

5. How stable are they financially?

6. Are there any major organizational problems?

7. Do employees like working for this organization?

8. What is the outlook for this field/industry in the next five years. (Is this industry in a stable, growth pattern or is it on a decline?)

To gain information on the organization that you are interested in, you can refer to publications such as:

❑ Better Business Bureau reports
❑ Chamber of Commerce information
❑ Dun and Bradstreet references
❑ Fitch Corporations Manuals
❑ Moody's Manuals
❑ Poor's Registry of Directors and Executives
❑ Standard and Poor's publications
❑ Thomas' Register of American Manufacturers, etc.

Many of these publications can be found at the public library (main branch). Other resources include a friend or relative who works for the company, a secretary or receptionist within the company, and people in competitive companies.

THE INTERVIEW

This section discusses the JOB INTERVIEW, undoubtedly one of the most critical parts of your job search.

Job interviews are structured so that the greatest exchange of information can take place in the least amount of time, often 20 or 30 minutes. It is comprised of four (4) distinct parts: the INTRODUCTION, BACKGROUND, DISCUSSION and the CLOSE.

1. **INTRODUCTION**

    First impressions and primary judgments are made at this point of the interview. The evaluation of your appearance, manner, maturity and enthusiasm starts the minute you enter. The way you shake the interviewer's hand, sit and talk all play a major part in the impression you make. Maintain good eye contact. Project sincerity, enthusiasm, competence, and confidence.

2. **BACKGROUND**

    During this point of the interview, the interviewer begins to evaluate your qualifications and suitability for employment at his/her company or organization. Using questions and answers, the interviewer notes how you handle yourself and tries to evaluate your maturity, self-confidence, personal values, ability to relate to others, in addition to your career ambition. As a result of this process, the interviewer's initial judgment of you might be revised or confirmed.

3. **DISCUSSION**

    It is here that you will be given the opportunity to ask questions and to sell yourself. Make sure that you have some knowledge of the company in order to discuss it intelligently. Failure to do your homework before an interview may cause you to lose a job prospect with the company.

    Be prepared to discuss such things as why you have chosen to apply at this particular company or organization, geographical preferences, company operations, and job responsibilities in your area of interest. The interviewer may initiate discussion of salary.

    Show how you can be of value to the company, department and/or position by presenting your qualifications as they relate to the particular position you are applying for. Use specific examples to:

    ❑ Show how you have used the required skills
    ❑ Bridge or link your skills to the requirements of the position. It is important to demonstrate how you can transfer your knowledge to meet the organization's needs.

    The DISCUSSION is a very critical part of the interview in that the interviewer is trying to determine if your qualifications will fit a particular job opening. Know your immediate and long-range career objectives.

4. **CLOSE**

    Try to "wrap up the interview in your favor", as the end of the interview is what the interviewer is most likely to recall about you. There are two points you must remember in order to develop a strong ending:

    1. Summarize your strengths and qualifications for the position. Relate how your skills, experience and other assets meet these qualification. Though you have probably already discussed this earlier in the interview, it is highly effective to leave the inter-

viewer with this summary clearly in mind. This "technique" gives you one last chance to "sell yourself."

2. Clarify how and when you will be notified of the hiring decision. Should you check back with the interviewer or will he/she notify you?

Express an interest in the position. Thank the interviewer for his/her time.

The interview is not over until you have sent a thank you note.

GENERAL INTERVIEWING TIPS

DO . . .

1. Prepare for your interview. FAILURE TO PREPARE IS LIKE PREPARING TO FAIL. Practice what you will say to various types of questions.

2. Dress well and appropriately. Many candidates are refused employment based on poor appearance and dress alone. Rule of thumb: Dress one "step up" from the attire worn for the position you seek. Pants, however, are not acceptable for women.

3. Arrive approximately 10 minutes early. Appearing or feeling rushed leaves a poor impression. Make sure that you have very explicit directions to the location of the interview.

4. Be aware of your body language. GOOD EYE CONTACT IS A MUST.

5. Remember the employer's or interviewer's name. Use it several times during the interview, especially at the close.

6. Give a firm (but not knuckle-cracker type) handshake. Limp handshakes can project weakness to the interviewer. Let the interviewer offer his/her hand first.

7. Ask for a business card to provide information for future correspondence such as a thank you note.

8. Send a thank you note. This will give you another opportunity to express your interest in the position and the company.

9. Wait until the interviewer offers you a chair before you sit down.

10. Adjust your communication style to match that of the interviewer. By doing this, you will enhance the rapport and "chemistry" between you and the interviewer. Approximately 80% of the impression you make is subjective and is a result of positive rapport or a lack thereof.

11. Wear a SMILE. This helps you establish positive rapport with the interviewer. Your facial expression can project interest and motivation.

12. Carry several copies of your resume. Your interviewer may not have yours in front of him/her during your interview.

13. Be pleasant and friendly, but businesslike.

14. Try to talk in terms of concrete experiences and give examples that demonstrate your point.

15. Be aware that the initial 30 seconds to three or four minutes has the potential to "make it or break it" for you. You don't want to have to play "catch up" for the rest of the interview.

16. Hesitate if you need time to adequately answer a question.

17. Ask questions during or at the end of the interview.

18. Allow the interviewer to control the interview.

19. Be "real". Be honest.

20. Let the interviewer decide when the interview is over. Ask when you will hear from him/her regarding the position or when you should call back.

21. Thank the interviewer for his/her time and consideration.

DON'T . . .

1. Be late for your interview.

2. Ask about salary, benefits or vacation time. Let the interviewer bring up the subject. It would be advisable to find out this information out ahead of time. Ask someone in Human Resources, a secretary or the person in charge of staffing to get this information for you.

3. Be critical of past employers, supervisors, or companies that you have worked with.

4. Hesitate to ask for a clarification of a specific question or point raised by the interviewer. This will also help you to gather your thoughts to answer the question.

5. Smoke or chew gum even if you are invited to do so.

6. Talk too much or ramble.

7. Apologize for any lack of experience. Counteract that lack by indicating a strong motivation and enthusiasm toward the job you are applying for.

8. Take any notes during the interview. It can be very distracting. (Taking down information such as names, dates, or telephone numbers is permissible.)

9. Try to be funny. A sense of humor is fine, but don't overdo it.

10. "Oversell" yourself. Be enthusiastic and interested, remembering that an "over-kill" can kill your chances of being hired.

11. Mention anything about your personal, domestic or financial problems. Discuss only matters that relate to the job.

12. Speak too softly. Doing so may make you appear meek.

13. Say you are applying because you need a job.

When asked "tough" questions, keep your answers brief and factual, such as reasons for leaving previous jobs. If you can, relate corporate decisions beyond your control such as:

❏ limited opportunity
❏ lack of meaningful work
❏ no authority
❏ low earnings

Maintain a constant interviewing demeanor—never apologize.

INTERVIEW QUESTIONS

Listed below are typical questions commonly asked in an interview. Keep in mind that the interviewer may be more interested in your *reaction* to some questions than in the *actual answers* you give.

1. **Tell me a little bit about your background and experience.**
2. In what type of position are you most interested?
3. **Where do you see yourself five years from now?**
4. What are your future vocational plans?
5. What led you to choose this particular field?
6. **How does the job that you are applying for relate to what you have done in the past?**
7. **Why do you think you would like to work for our company?**
8. **What do you know about our company?**
9. **What interests you about our product or service?**
10. **What do you consider to be your major strengths? What do you consider to be your major weaknesses? What do you do (or plan to do) to eliminate or temper your shortcomings?**
11. What can you contribute to our company that would make us want to hire you?
12. **Why should I hire you?**
13. How do you fit the requirements for this job?
14. What do you think it takes to be successful in a company like ours?
15. What one or two accomplishments have given you the most satisfaction?
16. What do you consider to be your greatest professional accomplishment?
17. What do you think has contributed most to the successes you have had?
18. How would you describe yourself?
19. Do you have any plans for continued study? An advanced degree?
20. In what kind of work environment are you most comfortable?
21. How do you work under pressure?
22. Do you have a geographical preference? Why?
23. Will you relocate? Does relocation bother you?
24. Are you willing to travel?
25. Are you willing to spend at least six months (or a year) as a trainee?
26. What jobs have you enjoyed the most? The least? Why?
27. What is your educational background?
28. What kind of people do you work with best?
29. What salary do you require?
30. Are there any questions that you want to ask?
31. What additional information do you think I should have about you?

Also be prepared to answer more pointed questions, such as:

1. Have you ever been fired? Asked to resign?
2. Why did you leave your last position?
3. Why have you changed jobs so often?
4. Why have you decided to change jobs at this time?
5. Who are your references? May I contact them?

Some questions may be *situational* in nature. Be prepared for the interviewer to ask how you would *handle* a particular work situation.

SAMPLE INTERVIEW QUESTIONS FOR TEACHERS

Some of these questions are "exploratory" or "informational" in nature. Others are hypothetical situation questions, asking you to tell how you would react or deal with specific issues. You may receive both types of questions in your interview.

1. What is your philosophy of education?

2. Describe your style of teaching.

3. Describe your student teaching experience.

4. With what kind of student do you most like to work? Least like to work?

5. What was the biggest problem you had while you were student teaching?

6. What do you do to individualize your teaching?

7. How would you provide for "rapid learners"?

8. Why do you want to teach?

9. How and when do you discipline a student?

10. How would you handle a student who continually "acted up" in class?

11. Describe the ideal classroom.

12. What would you do or how would you treat a student who refused to do the work you assigned?

13. Why should our school district hire you?

14. What do you know about our school district?

15. What grade level do you prefer? Why?

16. How would you work with students below grade level, especially low socioeconomic students?

17. What do you feel are the qualities of an excellent teacher?

18. What is the greatest attribute you can bring to a class of students?

19. What three words would you use to describe yourself as a teacher?

20. Are parent/teacher conferences important? Why or why not?

Additional suggestions for teachers are found on the following page.

Be Prepared . . .

    ❑ To discuss your professional views of grading, discipline, lesson planning and individualized instruction.

    ❑ To give your philosophy of education—a brief statement of your ideas on goals and purposes as a teacher.

    ❑ To discuss your student teaching experiences.

    ❑ To be conversant about testing, programs and curriculum in your field of specialization.

Most education interviews will be informal as opposed to formal in nature. Dress and act like a teacher.

QUESTIONS THE INTERVIEWEE MIGHT ASK DURING THE INTERVIEW

The following is a selection of questions that an interviewee might ask in an employment interview. It is important to ask questions to demonstrate your interest and enthusiasm, as well as a lead-in to information you wish to impart. The questions you ask show the interviewer more about yourself, the contributions you can make to the organization, and how much you know about the company. Your questions will help you to obtain information needed to evaluate the company and the job. Be careful not to ask a question already discussed during the interview. This gives the impression that you were not listening.

1. Would you describe the duties of this job for me?
2. What type of training is involved?
3. Could you show me where this job fits in the organization?
4. Is there anything unusually demanding about the job I should know about?
5. What is the company's promotion procedure?
6. What growth potential do you see for this job?
7. Could you tell me in what kind of environment I would be working?
8. Are employees afforded an opportunity for continuing education?
9. How much travel will be required?
10. Will relocation be necessary?
11. What are the opportunities for training and advancement? Interviewers are most impressed by questions like this that reveal some long-range planning and are a sign of drive and wanting to get ahead.
12. When will you be making a decision regarding this position?

Avoid asking the initial questions about salary and company benefits. The salary may not be established and some companies prefer to discuss these areas during a second interview.

If the employer finally says "NO," keep the door open and bridges unburned by asking:

    ❑ Do you know of other organizations who might be interested in my experience?

    ❑ I very much like what you are doing. Could you keep my resume on hand for other openings in your office?

    ❑ If the situation changes, would you please let me know?

Evaluate the interview as soon as possible. Before your impressions of the interview fade from your memory, examine the experience you have just been through.

Ask yourself these questions:

❑ How did the interview go in general?

❑ Was I adequately prepared for the interview? Did I know enough about the organization, it's products or services?

❑ What points did I make that seemed to interest the interviewer?

❑ Did I present my qualifications well?

❑ Did I act enthusiastic and optimistic?

❑ How can I improve my next interview? What would I do differently?

QUESTIONS THE INTERVIEWER ASKS HIMSELF/HERSELF ABOUT YOU

As mentioned earlier, the interviewer's task is to select the most qualified applicant for the position in question. Thus, during and after each interview, answers to the following questions, in one form or another, must be weighed.

Once you leave the interview, your task is just about over, but the interviewer still has the job of making a decision. If you are aware of the things the interviewer may ask himself/herself after you have gone, you can, by your words and actions during the interview try to make these answers favorable to yourself.

1. Is this person industrious and ambitious?
2. Will he/she be a loyal employee?
3. Does the applicant show initiative?
4. Does he/she seem open-minded?
5. Is the applicant enthusiastic?
6. Does the applicant talk too much?
7. Does the interviewee have the capacity to learn?
8. Does the applicant seem to have good common sense?
9. Will he/she be a good team worker?
10. Will this applicant fit in with our employees?
11. If I give this person a job, will he/she stick with it?
12. Does this person seem thorough?
13. Does the applicant appear to want to give TO the job as much as he/she wants to get a paycheck?

WHY APPLICANTS "STRIKE OUT" IN THE INTERVIEW

Note:

See "GENERAL INTERVIEWING TIPS." Many of the following comments relate to the suggestions in that section. This list was extracted from a survey of companies who were questioned as to why an applicant who is capable of doing the job is **not** hired by them.

1. Poor personal appearance.
2. Lack of interest and enthusiasm, passive, indifferent.
3. Over-emphasis on salary, benefits and compensation.
4. Failure to look the interviewer in the eye.
5. Limp, fishy handshake.
6. Unwillingness to go where sent.
7. Late to the interview.
8. Asks no questions about the job.
9. Indefinite response to specific questions.
10. Overbearing, over aggressive, conceited "know it all" complex.
11. Inability to express oneself clearly. Poor diction, grammar.
12. No purpose or goals. Lack of career planning.
13. Lack of confidence, ill at ease.
14. Lack of knowledge of field of specialization.
15. Unwilling to start at bottom. Expects too much too soon.
16. Makes excuses, evasive.
17. Lack of tact and maturity.
18. Lack of manners, courtesy.
19. Lack of vitality.
20. Indecision.
21. Merely shopping around.
22. Interested in job only temporarily.
23. No interest in company or industry.
24. Cynical.
25. Low moral standards.
26. Lazy.
27. Strong prejudices and intolerant behavior. Radical ideas.
28. Narrow interests.
29. High pressure type.
30. Condemnation of past employers/companies.

SALARY NEGOTIATIONS

Before you negotiate a salary, ask yourself the following questions:

- ❏ Is this the position I want?
- ❏ Does this environment suit me?
- ❏ Will I be comfortable working with the people at this agency or business?

If the answer is *yes,* then consider the following information before negotiating the salary:

1. **Salary is often renegotiable.** Even when there is a set range, some negotiation is often possible.

2. **Know your strengths and level of experience and put a dollar value on these two factors.** Most people never look at their strengths and uniqueness. Before you negotiate a salary, it is very helpful to list all your strengths.

3. **Research the local market to determine comparable salaries.** This will allow you to renegotiate with greater confidence.

4. **Negotiate 10–15% higher than your current and/or acceptable salary.** Set your goals high. Studies show that those who set higher goals get more.

5. **Get the other side to make the first offer.** There are many risks involved being the first to mention a salary figure. By doing so, you may:

   ❑ cut off a whole range of what's negotiable. Once the applicant mentions a figure any further negotiation upwards becomes impossible.

   ❑ disqualify yourself by mentioning a figure significantly higher than the employer's salary range.

   ❑ end up with a salary lower than what the employer intended to offer.

   If asked to state an acceptable salary, turn around the question by asking what **salary range** they are considering. Your strengths and level of experience will help you determine where you fit in that range.

6. **Never accept the first offer.** You have asked for more than your acceptable salary giving yourself "room" to negotiate. Link your strengths to their needs. Concede slowly and in small increments. In negotiation, patience is important.

7. **Weigh salary decisions carefully.** Take into consideration the company's benefit package, stock options, bonuses, vacation policies, raise schedule and cost of living adjustments, and advancement possibility.

8. **If possible, take at least 24–48 hours to consider the offer.** Renegotiate if the offer that you are given does not meet your needs. Do **not allow** yourself to be pressured.

INTERVIEW PREPARATION SHEET

1. Data and time of interview.

2. Address.

3. Name of interviewer and his/her title.

4. Position title.

5. Why am I interested in this particular position?

6. What do I know about the product/service and company in general?

7. What is the job description?

8. What skills, experience, and qualifications are required for this position?

9. Which of the above can I match?

10. What do I lack?

11. In what way can I compensate for what I lack?

12. What special strengths and qualities can I bring to this organization and particular position?

13. What questions can I ask during the interview to gain information and project both motivation and enthusiasm?

    a. _____
    _____
    _____

    b. _____
    _____
    _____

    c. _____
    _____
    _____

    d. _____
    _____
    _____

14. Where do you see yourself in 5 years?

    _____
    _____

8

CAREER PATHING

How can I get from where I am today to a specific job or position within my organization? How can I achieve the career success that I desire? Though it is obvious that there is not only one answer to these questions, the concept of career paths or career pathing can be considered one of the important "spokes in the wheel" for career happiness and success.

A career path is the plan that you develop to give direction to your career. Career pathing is very important to a company and their employees because it promotes both growth and stability. Developing and implementing a career path plan can both enhance your job satisfaction and utilize the staff of a business more effectively.

INDIVIDUAL CAREER PATHING

To develop your individual career path, identify the position you presently hold, the position or work situation you would like to hold in five (5) or six (6) years (your long-term goal), and the positions you will need to hold in between now and your long-term goal. What work situations or positions can you put yourself in that have the potential to lead you to your goal?

All career moves do not need to be upward or result in advancement in salary, title or responsibility. Would you take a small cut in pay, move to a new company and new position if the move, in the long run, would provide an increased opportunity for career growth and job satisfaction? A well thought out plan may lead you to take a lateral or downward path that has the potential to increase your skills and marketability and, thus, open up new opportunities for you within your career. In developing your career path, take into account both short and long-term planning.

CAREER PATHING WITHIN ORGANIZATIONS

Many organizations have a formalized and written career pathing chart that enables employees to easily identify the steps or positions they might take to reach a specific position or goal. This system is often referred to as a "career ladder" and is available to employees through the Human Resources or Personnel Department. Because career ladders imply upward mobility only, it is more limiting than individual career pathing. As previously indicated, in personal career pathing, you may backstep or take a lateral move to increase skills and growth within a given field.

INDIVIDUAL
CAREER PATHING OPTIONS

The following illustrations provide examples of vertical, lateral and digressional career paths.

Vertical

Lateral

Digressional

**Lateral/Vertical
Career Growth**

**Digressional/Vertical
Career Growth**

9

FORMS

WORKSITE INFORMATION SHEET
Career Work Experience

Name _____ Class and time _____

Agency or business chosen _____

Agency or business address _____

           (City) _____ (Zip Code) _____

Name of Supervisor/Individual you report to _____

Phone number(s) _____

1. Describe the function of your agency/business (What do they do?)

_____

_____

_____

2. Why did you choose this worksite?

_____

_____

_____

3. List your beginning and projected responsibilities for the field work experience. Identify those that you will be doing in the beginning, the middle and toward the end. (Use back side of sheet if needed.)

_____

_____

_____

_____

_____

_____

_____

_____

WORKSITE INFORMATION SHEET
Career Work Experience

Name _____ Class and time _____

Agency or business chosen _____

Agency or business address _____

           (City) _____ (Zip code) _____

Name of Supervisor/Individual you report to _____

Phone number(s) _____

   1. Describe the function of your agency/business (What do they do?)

      _____

      _____

      _____

   2. Why did you choose this worksite?

      _____

      _____

      _____

   3. List your beginning and projected responsibilities for the field work experience. Identify those that you will be doing in the beginning, the middle and toward the end. (Use back side of sheet if needed.)

      _____

      _____

      _____

      _____

      _____

      _____

      _____

MIDTERM EVALUATION

Name of student_____ Date _____

Business or agency _____

Address _____ City _____ Zip_____

Supervisor _____ Phone _____

Check the statement that best describes the student named above.

Reliability

____ Extremely reliable
____ Above average in reliability
____ Average
____ Often undependable
____ Completely undependable

Relations with others on the job

____ Accepted exceptionally well by others
____ Above average in relations with others
____ Works satisfactorily with others
____ Exhibits some difficulty working with others
____ Does not work well with others

Decision Making

____ Exceptionally good judgment and decision making skills
____ Makes very good decisions
____ Average in making decisions
____ Makes poor decisions often
____ Consistently makes poor decisions

Attitude, enthusiasm and industriousness

____ Student is highly enthusiastic and industrious
____ Student is above average in this area
____ Student's attitude appears average
____ Student's attitude is somewhat indifferent
____ Student exhibits a poor attitude

Quality of work performed

____ Excellent
____ Very good
____ Average
____ Below average
____ Poor

Overall or general evaluation of student

____ Excellent
____ Above average
____ Average
____ Below average
____ Poor

SEE OTHER SIDE FOR ADDITIONAL EVALUATION AND COMMENTS

It is important to the student to have your personal comments and suggestions.

Personal comments from student's supervisor: _____

_____

_____

_____

_____

_____

_____

_____

_____

_____

_____

Suggestions for student:_____

_____

_____

_____

_____

_____

_____

_____

SUPERVISOR'S SIGNATURE _____

MIDTERM EVALUATION

Name of student_____ Date _____

Business or agency _____

Address _____ City _____ Zip_____

Supervisor _____ Phone _____

Check the statement that best describes the student named above.

Reliability

____ Extremely reliable
____ Above average in reliability
____ Average
____ Often undependable
____ Completely undependable

Relations with others on the job

____ Accepted exceptionally well by others
____ Above average in relations with others
____ Works satisfactorily with others
____ Exhibits some difficulty working with others
____ Does not work well with others

Decision Making

____ Exceptionally good judgment and decision making skills
____ Makes very good decisions
____ Average in making decisions
____ Makes poor decisions often
____ Consistently makes poor decisions

Attitude, enthusiasm and industriousness

____ Student is highly enthusiastic and industrious
____ Student is above average in this area
____ Student's attitude appears average
____ Student's attitude is somewhat indifferent
____ Student exhibits a poor attitude

Quality of work performed

____ Excellent
____ Very good
____ Average
____ Below average
____ Poor

Overall or general evaluation of student

____ Excellent
____ Above average
____ Average
____ Below average
____ Poor

**SEE OTHER SIDE FOR ADDITIONAL
EVALUATION AND COMMENTS**

151

It is important to the student to have your personal comments and suggestions.

Personal comments from student's supervisor: _____

_____

_____

_____

_____

_____

_____

_____

_____

Suggestions for student:_____

_____

_____

_____

_____

_____

_____

SUPERVISOR'S SIGNATURE _____

FINAL EVALUATION

Name of student_____ Date _____

Business or agency _____

Address _____ City _____ Zip_____

Supervisor _____ Phone _____

Check the statement that best describes the student named above.

Reliability

____ Extremely reliable
____ Above average in reliability
____ Average
____ Often undependable
____ Completely undependable

Relations with others on the job

____ Accepted exceptionally well by others
____ Above average in relations with others
____ Works satisfactorily with others
____ Exhibits some difficulty working with others
____ Does not work well with others

Decision Making

____ Exceptionally good judgment and decision making skills
____ Makes very good decisions
____ Average in making decisions
____ Makes poor decisions often
____ Consistently makes poor decisions

Attitude, enthusiasm and industriousness

____ Student is highly enthusiastic and industrious
____ Student is above average in this area
____ Student's attitude appears average
____ Student's attitude is somewhat indifferent
____ Student exhibits a poor attitude

Quality of work performed

____ Excellent
____ Very good
____ Average
____ Below average
____ Poor

Overall or general evaluation of student

____ Excellent
____ Above average
____ Average
____ Below average
____ Poor

**SEE OTHER SIDE FOR ADDITIONAL
EVALUATION AND COMMENTS**

It is important to the student to have your personal comments and suggestions.

Personal comments from student's supervisor: _____

_____

_____

_____

_____

_____

_____

_____

_____

_____

_____

Suggestions for student:_____

_____

_____

_____

_____

_____

_____

_____

SUPERVISOR'S SIGNATURE _____

FINAL EVALUATION

Name of student _____ Date _____

Business or agency _____

Address _____ City _____ Zip_____

Supervisor _____ Phone _____

Check the statement that best describes the student named above.

Reliability

____ Extremely reliable
____ Above average in reliability
____ Average
____ Often undependable
____ Completely undependable

Relations with others on the job

____ Accepted exceptionally well by others
____ Above average in relations with others
____ Works satisfactorily with others
____ Exhibits some difficulty working with others
____ Does not work well with others

Decision Making

____ Exceptionally good judgment and decision making skills
____ Makes very good decisions
____ Average in making decisions
____ Makes poor decisions often
____ Consistently makes poor decisions

Attitude, enthusiasm and industriousness

____ Student is highly enthusiastic and industrious
____ Student is above average in this area
____ Student's attitude appears average
____ Student's attitude is somewhat indifferent
____ Student exhibits a poor attitude

Quality of work performed

____ Excellent
____ Very good
____ Average
____ Below average
____ Poor

Overall or general evaluation of student

____ Excellent
____ Above average
____ Average
____ Below average
____ Poor

SEE OTHER SIDE FOR ADDITIONAL EVALUATION AND COMMENTS

155

It is important to the student to have your personal comments and suggestions.

Personal comments from student's supervisor: _____

_____

_____

_____

_____

_____

_____

_____

_____

_____

_____

_____

Suggestions for student:_____

_____

_____

_____

_____

_____

_____

_____

SUPERVISOR'S SIGNATURE _____

RECORD OF FIELD WORK HOURS

Student's name_____ Class day & time_____

Business or Agency_____

Supervisor_____

Instructions: Field work credit cannot be given to a student without verification of hours worked at the site. To assure accurate records, it is suggested that BOTH the STUDENT and the SUPERVISOR record the number of hours worked on a weekly basis. THE SUPERVISOR SHOULD SIGN EACH WEEKLY RECORD AT THE TOP OF EACH BOX. The student will turn in their record of field work hours at the end of the semester.

*Signature*_____

DAYS	S	M	T	W	Th	F	S
DATE							
HOURS							
Total number of hours							

*Signature*_____

DAYS	S	M	T	W	Th	F	S
DATE							
HOURS							
Total number of hours							

*Signature*_____

DAYS	S	M	T	W	Th	F	S
DATE							
HOURS							
Total number of hours							

*Signature*_____

DAYS	S	M	T	W	Th	F	S
DATE							
HOURS							
Total number of hours							

*Signature*_____

DAYS	S	M	T	W	Th	F	S
DATE							
HOURS							
Total number of hours							

*Signature*_____

DAYS	S	M	T	W	Th	F	S
DATE							
HOURS							
Total number of hours							

*Signature*_____

DAYS	S	M	T	W	Th	F	S
DATE							
HOURS							
Total number of hours							

*Signature*_____

DAYS	S	M	T	W	Th	F	S
DATE							
HOURS							
Total number of hours							

*Signature*_____

DAYS	S	M	T	W	Th	F	S
DATE							
HOURS							
Total number of hours							

*Signature*_____

DAYS	S	M	T	W	Th	F	S
DATE							
HOURS							
Total number of hours							

*Signature*_____

DAYS	S	M	T	W	Th	F	S
DATE							
HOURS							
Total number of hours							

*Signature*_____

DAYS	S	M	T	W	Th	F	S
DATE							
HOURS							
Total number of hours							

*Signature*_____

DAYS	S	M	T	W	Th	F	S
DATE							
HOURS							
Total number of hours							

*Signature*_____

DAYS	S	M	T	W	Th	F	S
DATE							
HOURS							
Total number of hours							

_____
Supervisor's Signature

RECORD OF FIELD WORK HOURS

Student's name_____ Class day & time_____

Business or Agency_____

Supervisor_____

Instructions: Field work credit cannot be given to a student without verification of hours worked at the site. To assure accurate records, it is suggested that BOTH the STUDENT and the SUPERVISOR record the number of hours worked on a weekly basis. THE SUPERVISOR SHOULD SIGN EACH WEEKLY RECORD AT THE TOP OF EACH BOX. The student will turn in their record of field work hours at the end of the semester.

*Signature*_____

DAYS	S	M	T	W	Th	F	S
DATE							
HOURS							
Total number of hours							

*Signature*_____

DAYS	S	M	T	W	Th	F	S
DATE							
HOURS							
Total number of hours							

*Signature*_____

DAYS	S	M	T	W	Th	F	S
DATE							
HOURS							
Total number of hours							

*Signature*_____

DAYS	S	M	T	W	Th	F	S
DATE							
HOURS							
Total number of hours							

*Signature*_____

DAYS	S	M	T	W	Th	F	S
DATE							
HOURS							
Total number of hours							

*Signature*_____

DAYS	S	M	T	W	Th	F	S
DATE							
HOURS							
Total number of hours							

*Signature*_____

DAYS	S	M	T	W	Th	F	S
DATE							
HOURS							
Total number of hours							

*Signature*_____

DAYS	S	M	T	W	Th	F	S
DATE							
HOURS							
Total number of hours							

*Signature*_____

DAYS	S	M	T	W	Th	F	S
DATE							
HOURS							
Total number of hours							

*Signature*_____

DAYS	S	M	T	W	Th	F	S
DATE							
HOURS							
Total number of hours							

*Signature*_____

DAYS	S	M	T	W	Th	F	S
DATE							
HOURS							
Total number of hours							

*Signature*_____

DAYS	S	M	T	W	Th	F	S
DATE							
HOURS							
Total number of hours							

*Signature*_____

DAYS	S	M	T	W	Th	F	S
DATE							
HOURS							
Total number of hours							

*Signature*_____

DAYS	S	M	T	W	Th	F	S
DATE							
HOURS							
Total number of hours							

_____
Supervisor's Signature

10

GUIDELINES FOR COOPERATING BUSINESSES AND AGENCIES

CAREER WORK EXPERIENCE PROGRAM
OVERVIEW

Many students are undecided about their career goals and courses and need some knowledge, experience or investigation to help them make a career decision. Others wish to enter the work world for the first time but learn that it is often difficult to obtain employment without actual work experience. Still other students may be dissatisfied with their present job or career and wish to explore other options. These critically important needs can be met by the course CAREER WORK EXPERIENCE which helps students gain work experience, on-the-job training and exploration of a work environment by volunteering to work in a business or agency of their choice.

Students **attend** one class per week for 4 weeks. The class sessions focus on CAREER DEVELOPMENT. Topics include resume writing, interviewing skills, and job-search strategies.

Students **work** in a business or agency of their choice. This is done on a volunteer basis. Students **arrange** work experience time according to the number of semester credits they wish to earn. The actual work time is decided upon between the students and their supervisors. Students are evaluated by their supervisor both at midterm and at the end of the semester.

CAREER WORK EXPERIENCE COURSE OBJECTIVES

This program's primary objective is to enhance the student's career development. This is accomplished by giving students the opportunity to explore the world of work and receive experience and skills within local businesses and agencies.

Additional objectives are:

❑ To help students determine whether their aptitudes and interests are compatible with their educational and career goals.

❑ To enhance students' self-marketing skills.

❑ To promote the setting of career goals.

❑ To demonstrate the vital relationship between college courses and the real work world through the concept of volunteerism.

CAREER WORK EXPERIENCE can be described as a *win-win* program. The students ''win'' as a result of their career growth. Cooperating businesses and agencies ''win'' because of the dedication, work and time donated to them by the students.

CAREER WORK EXPERIENCE COURSE REQUIREMENTS

The following are Career Work Experience course requirements. Students are expected to:

1. Attend the classroom portion of the course.

2. Choose a corporation, business or agency where they will volunteer a set number of hours weekly during the semester.

3. Select a work schedule that is satisfactory to both student and field work supervisor.

4. Turn in required assignments.

5. Keep careful records of field work attendance. Give duplicate field work attendance form to supervisor.

6. Turn in midterm evaluation half-way through the semester and a final evaluation at the semester's end.

7. Turn in signed attendance forms to complete and receive credit for the course.

8. Arrange several meetings with supervisor to evaluate student's work.

SUGGESTIONS TO SUPERVISORS

Thank you for allowing our students to volunteer within your business or agency. This experience may have an important impact upon this student's career development and your cooperation and support is very much appreciated.

Our student is coming to you to explore a career and/or gain skills and experience in a given area or field. In order to tap the valuable resources this student has to offer and make best use of their time, it may help you to keep the following suggestions in mind:

1. Students will have met with you for an interview prior to volunteering with your business or agency. A specific job description or work plan may have been determined at that time. If not, it is important for both the student and supervisor to develop a WORK PLAN that will benefit BOTH the student and the business. Knowledge of the student's expectations, skills, and education will aid in the formulation of a good work plan or job description.

2. Students want to be challenged. They want to feel a sense of accomplishment and see results. Within your own realm, taking in consideration the student's skills, try to give him (or her) as much responsibility as possible. The more responsibility they are given, the more dedicated and motivated they will become, and, thus, do the best job for you.

3. The success of your experience and the experience of the student depends, in part, on your planning, guidance and supervision. The supervisor need NOT continuously work with the student. However, it is important, especially in the beginning, to give enough guidance, supervision and explanations that enables the student to do the very best job possible.

4. It is recommended that you schedule occasional evaluation interviews throughout the semester. The student will benefit from receiving an evaluation of their work.

5. All Career Work Experience students are extremely interested in their careers and career growth. Many will ask a variety of questions while exploring or gaining skills and experience in a given field. It is highly recommended that you discuss this topic with the student and give guide-

lines on when, how and where questions can be asked. Students truly appreciate a willingness on your part to enhance their career growth.

6. Invite the student to attend one or more staff meetings. "Behind the scenes" information can be invaluable to students' learning.

7. At the beginning of the semester, introduce the student to the business or agency as a whole. To do this, it is suggested that you:

   ❑ Give a tour of the facility.
   ❑ Introduce him/her to other workers.
   ❑ Describe your business or agency goals.
   ❑ Give information on the clientele you serve, services you offer, or products you make.
   ❑ Introduce the student to any materials and information he/she may need (or need to know about) in order to work effectively.

8. Constantly check if you are making MAXIMUM use of your student volunteer.

9. Be aware of the written evaluation and time sheet deadlines. (The student will give you this information.) Fill out *both* sides of the evaluation forms, sign and give them to the student in a SEALED envelope. The marks will be given on an A, B, C, D, F basis.

   ❑ A = Excellent
   ❑ B = Good
   ❑ C = Average
   ❑ D = Below average
   ❑ F = Unsatisfactory

10. If a student's performance is unsatisfactory, please consult with the program coordinator for the **CAREER WORK EXPERIENCE** course.

WORKSITE INFORMATION SHEET
Career Work Experience

Name _____ Class and time _____

Agency or business chosen _____

Agency or business address _____

(City) _____ (Zip code) _____

Name of Supervisor/Individual you report to _____

Phone number(s) _____

1. Describe the function of your agency/business (What do they do?)

   _____

   _____

   _____

2. Why did you choose this worksite?

   _____

   _____

   _____

3. List your beginning and projected responsibilities for the field work experience. Identify those that you will be doing in the beginning, the middle and toward the end. (Use back side of sheet if needed.)

   _____

   _____

   _____

   _____

   _____

   _____

   _____

MIDTERM EVALUATION

Name of student_____ Date _____

Business or agency _____

Address _____ City _____ Zip_____

Supervisor _____ Phone _____

Check the statement that best describes the student named above.

Reliability

____ Extremely reliable
____ Above average in reliability
____ Average
____ Often undependable
____ Completely undependable

Relations with others on the job

____ Accepted exceptionally well by others
____ Above average in relations with others
____ Works satisfactorily with others
____ Exhibits some difficulty working with others
____ Does not work well with others

Decision Making

____ Exceptionally good judgment and decision making skills
____ Makes very good decisions
____ Average in making decisions
____ Makes poor decisions often
____ Consistently makes poor decisions

Attitude, enthusiasm and industriousness

____ Student is highly enthusiastic and industrious
____ Student is above average in this area
____ Student's attitude appears average
____ Student's attitude is somewhat indifferent
____ Student exhibits a poor attitude

Quality of work performed

____ Excellent
____ Very good
____ Average
____ Below average
____ Poor

Overall or general evaluation of student

____ Excellent
____ Above average
____ Average
____ Below average
____ Poor

SEE OTHER SIDE FOR ADDITIONAL EVALUATION AND COMMENTS

It is important to the student to have your personal comments and suggestions.

Personal comments from student's supervisor: _____

_____

_____

_____

_____

_____

_____

_____

_____

_____

_____

Suggestions for student:_____

_____

_____

_____

_____

_____

_____

_____

SUPERVISOR'S SIGNATURE _____

FINAL EVALUATION

Name of student_____ Date _____

Business or agency _____

Address _____ City _____ Zip_____

Supervisor _____ Phone _____

Check the statement that best describes the student named above.

Reliability

____ Extremely reliable
____ Above average in reliability
____ Average
____ Often undependable
____ Completely undependable

Relations with others on the job

____ Accepted exceptionally well by others
____ Above average in relations with others
____ Works satisfactorily with others
____ Exhibits some difficulty working with others
____ Does not work well with others

Decision Making

____ Exceptionally good judgment and decision making skills
____ Makes very good decisions
____ Average in making decisions
____ Makes poor decisions often
____ Consistently makes poor decisions

Attitude, enthusiasm and industriousness

____ Student is highly enthusiastic and industrious
____ Student is above average in this area
____ Student's attitude appears average
____ Student's attitude is somewhat indifferent
____ Student exhibits a poor attitude

Quality of work performed

____ Excellent
____ Very good
____ Average
____ Below average
____ Poor

Overall or general evaluation of student

____ Excellent
____ Above average
____ Average
____ Below average
____ Poor

SEE OTHER SIDE FOR ADDITIONAL EVALUATION AND COMMENTS

It is important to the student to have your personal comments and suggestions.

Personal comments from student's supervisor: _____

_____

_____

_____

_____

_____

_____

_____

_____

_____

_____

_____

Suggestions for student:_____

_____

_____

_____

_____

_____

_____

_____

SUPERVISOR'S SIGNATURE _____

RECORD OF FIELD WORK HOURS

Student's name_____ Class day & time_____

Business or Agency_____

Supervisor_____

Instructions: Field work credit cannot be given to a student without verification of hours worked at the site. To assure accurate records, it is suggested that BOTH the STUDENT and the SUPERVISOR record the number of hours worked on a weekly basis. THE SUPERVISOR SHOULD SIGN EACH WEEKLY RECORD AT THE TOP OF EACH BOX. The student will turn in their record of field work hours at the end of the semester.

*Signature*_____

DAYS	S	M	T	W	Th	F	S
DATE							
HOURS							
Total number of hours							

*Signature*_____

DAYS	S	M	T	W	Th	F	S
DATE							
HOURS							
Total number of hours							

*Signature*_____

DAYS	S	M	T	W	Th	F	S
DATE							
HOURS							
Total number of hours							

*Signature*_____

DAYS	S	M	T	W	Th	F	S
DATE							
HOURS							
Total number of hours							

*Signature*_____

DAYS	S	M	T	W	Th	F	S
DATE							
HOURS							
Total number of hours							

*Signature*_____

DAYS	S	M	T	W	Th	F	S
DATE							
HOURS							
Total number of hours							

Signature_____

DAYS	S	M	T	W	Th	F	S
DATE							
HOURS							
Total number of hours							

Signature_____

DAYS	S	M	T	W	Th	F	S
DATE							
HOURS							
Total number of hours							

Signature_____

DAYS	S	M	T	W	Th	F	S
DATE							
HOURS							
Total number of hours							

Signature_____

DAYS	S	M	T	W	Th	F	S
DATE							
HOURS							
Total number of hours							

Signature_____

DAYS	S	M	T	W	Th	F	S
DATE							
HOURS							
Total number of hours							

Signature_____

DAYS	S	M	T	W	Th	F	S
DATE							
HOURS							
Total number of hours							

_____
Supervisor's Signature